# ROD PARSLEY

# IDOLATRY
# —— IN ——
# AMERICA

# ROD PARSLEY

# IDOLATRY
## — IN —
# AMERICA

CHARISMA
HOUSE

While the author has made every effort to provide accurate, up-to-date source information at the time of publication, statistics and other data are constantly updated. Neither the publisher nor the author assumes any responsibility for errors or for changes that occur after publication. Further, the publisher and author do not have any control over and do not assume any responsibility for third-party websites or their content.

For more resources like this, visit charismahouse.com and the author's website at rodparsley.com.

Cataloging-in-Publication Data is on file with the Library of Congress.
International Standard Book Number: 978-1-63641-371-6
E-book ISBN: 978-1-63641-372-3

1 2023
Printed in the United States of America

Most Charisma Media products are available at special quantity discounts for bulk purchase for sales promotions, premiums, fund-raising, and educational needs. For details, call us at (407) 333-0600 or visit our website at www.charismamedia.com.

# CONTENTS

# INTRODUCTION

*Little children, keep yourselves from idols.*
—1 JOHN 5:21

*The whole land is filled with idols, and the
people are madly in love with them.*
—JEREMIAH 50:38, NLT

I N THE OPENING passage we have a portion of the
prophetic judgment that Jeremiah proclaimed over the
mighty Babylonian empire at its crescendo of prominence. Babylon overcame its neighbors and subsumed
them into itself as it metastasized into an ancient world
power. As its empire expanded, the only thing that
surpassed its appetite was its hubris. Babylon's tentacles
eventually reached the Judean hills, reducing Judah to
a vassal state before destroying it entirely (587/586 BC),
including its capital, Jerusalem, and its first temple,
which King Solomon had constructed in 957 BC.

Jeremiah had prophesied in Judah for years regarding
the consequences of rejecting Jehovah God and disobey-
ing His commandments. When he saw his prophecies
fulfilled, Jeremiah was unable to rejoice. Never before

had a seer been so undone by witnessing the accuracy and specificity of his prophetic utterances. The prophet could but weep as he witnessed his fellow Judeans perish in battle, die of starvation, succumb to disease, or limp away as prisoners of war to Babylonian captivity. It did not have to be this way. They could have heeded the voice of God in His passionate pleadings.

Jeremiah was rejected and despised by the very people to whom God had sent him. His enemies falsely accused him, abused him, arrested him, and imprisoned him. They were narrowly kept from killing him—and they would have, had the Babylonians not taken Jerusalem first. In an ironic twist of circumstance, the captain of the Babylonian guard released Jeremiah from the chains in which his own countrymen had bound him.

Despite all this, Jeremiah's dedication to his people never wavered. Although he was offered safety and provision in Babylon, he did not go. Rather, he chose to stay with those who remained in Judah under the authority of a governor chosen by the Babylonians. Subsequent events brought Jeremiah to Egypt, where he eventually received and delivered a word of righteous condemnation against the Babylonian empire that had stretched out its hand against the apple of God's eye.

A major cause of Babylon's downfall was the proliferation of idols within its borders, largely because of the aggregation of people groups from numerous lands who were brought to Babylon as captives and carried with them their own forms of worship. As Babylon continued to expand, it prospered above any nation or empire that preceded it. The conquests continued. The influence increased. It was the best of times, and it seemed it would last forever—until the entire enterprise crashed under the weight of its own corruption.

The official object of worship in Babylon was the god Marduk. Seven other deities were also commonly worshipped, as well as other, less prominent gods. Babylon was indeed filled with idols.

As for the "madly in love" factor mentioned by Jeremiah, consider these words from Daniel 5:1–4:

> Belshazzar the king made a great feast for a thousand of his lords and drank wine before the thousand. While he tasted the wine, Belshazzar commanded that they bring in the golden and silver vessels which his father Nebuchadnezzar had taken from the temple which was in Jerusalem, so that the king, and his officials, his wives, and his concubines might drink from them. Then they brought the golden vessels that were taken out of the temple of the house of God which was at Jerusalem. And the king and his officials, his wives and his concubines drank from them. They drank wine and praised the gods of gold and of silver, of bronze, of iron, of wood, and of stone.

The degeneracy of Belshazzar and his companions is on open display here. It was not good enough for them to limit their revelry to using ordinary vessels out of which they could drink their alcohol. The king insisted on using the vessels that were stolen from the temple in Jerusalem—vessels that had been created and consecrated holy for use in worship of the true God of heaven and earth.

It was at this time that handwriting appeared on the wall of the banquet hall. The bewildered king summoned Daniel to read the writing that had confounded the assembled pundits and prognosticators. Daniel reported the message sent from heaven, which sounded an alarm of imminent judgment upon Belshazzar and all those who joined the king in his drunken debauchery.

In its incarnation during the time of Daniel, the Babylonian empire lasted for approximately eighty years. It was destroyed because of its affinity for idolatry. Belshazzar was having a party, drinking toasts to the gods of wood and stone while his enemies were occupying his capital city. The mighty walls of Babylon had been designed to protect the city from external threats. Neither those walls nor the Babylonian pantheon of false gods could protect the revelers from the corrosion of corruption that had hollowed out their idolatrous hearts.

It is my intention to make clear that Jeremiah's dire warning applies to the current culture of contemporary America. It causes my heart deep distress to report that, like ancient Babylon, our nation is drowning in a veritable ocean of idols and—make no mistake—the people are madly in love with them. This derangement threatens to destroy and dismantle the very foundation stones of morality, family, and community upon which this nation was built and by which it has been sustained. We are in mortal danger. The threat against us is not from an external enemy but from a vast and accelerating spiritual void that provides no guidance, no answers, and no hope for the adversarial forces we now face.

I did not say there was no answer; there is. But that answer will never be discovered in any further pursuit of the false gods catapulted to prominence in our culture. Idols litter the landscape, parade across platforms, peer from tabloid pages, seduce on social media sites, manifest through music, and revel in religion. With great purpose and effect they insert themselves into our daily lives by any and all means at their demonic disposal.

Idols require attention, and then they abandon those who give them the attention they crave. They promise the rainbow but only deliver the rain. They demand a sacrifice of an unceasing supply of devotion and attention, finances, and effort. However, these false gods give their worshippers little or nothing in return other than empty promises.

The sin to which nations so easily fall prey is idolatry, which stops natural rain. However, the most serious consequence of idolatry throughout the ages has never been a lack of natural rain, as devastating as that can be. Listen to another prophet's description of idolatry's pernicious influence. Amos 8:11 says, "The time is coming, says the Lord GOD, when I will send a famine on the land, not a famine of bread, nor a thirst for water, but of hearing the words of the LORD."

The effects of natural drought are easy enough to see. Every week, the National Drought Mitigation Center updates a drought monitor map for the United States and its protectorates. In the recent past, headlines high-lighted extreme drought conditions that reduced the levels of rivers and reservoirs to historic lows and caused natural lakes to recede at alarming rates. What is even more concerning is that underground water reserves are diminished during droughts, and aquifers that provide water to millions can be depleted.

A famine of rain is only a symptom of a deeper prob-lem. What if there was a spiritual drought monitor for nations? What designation would America have? What about a drought map for individuals? How would your heart appear? Would it be normal, reflecting an abun-dance of spiritual resources, or would it be abnormally dry—or even register as being in a condition of excep-tional drought? How can it be that so many people are dry and dusty when the Word of God is available in more ways than ever before?

It is easy, from our distance in time and space from the ancient world, to point fingers of self-righteous accusation at other civilizations. We affirm that we would never fall prey to the same dangers. History proves otherwise. Human beings face the same difficul-ties regardless of country, culture, skin color, age group, or any of the other distinctions some are using so effec-tively to divide us.

Without a radical transformation, idolatry will always be a temptation—and as current events prove, a very tantalizing one. The only difference is that modern idols masquerade in many more disguises than the ancient ones. Not only that, but so-called sophisticated moderns have exceeded traditional idolatrous norms and have elevated the basest of impulses and the most foolish of behaviors to deity status. The pantheon of gods is apparently without limit—as are the ways to worship them— in our postmodern and even post-Christian world.

We must become weary of the vain pursuit, worn out from the smoke-and-mirror attractions idols offer. Then and only then will we seek the resolution to our personal and national problems in the only place it can truly be found. Before I tell you where that is, I will expose some of the most captivating and devastating categories of American idols.

# Chapter 1

# INFLUENCED: THE CULT OF CELEBRITY

*In the future, everyone will be world-famous for 15 minutes.*
—PONTUS HULTÉN, 1967

*For we dare not count or compare ourselves with those who commend themselves. They who measure themselves by one another and compare themselves with one another are not wise.*
—2 CORINTHIANS 10:12

MISS MORTENSON WAS like most young ladies of her generation, working in a factory to supply the endless demands of a nation at war while so many men were deployed overseas defending America's freedom. It was a series of particularly torturous twists of fate that caused her to become one of the most iconic celebrities in American history. A generation after her untimely death at only thirty-six years of age, nearly everyone still recognizes the name Marilyn Monroe.

He was a down-on-his-luck truck driver for an electric company, making $40 a week.[1] He had already made several unsuccessful attempts at becoming involved in the entertainment industry. His audition for a quartet had gone down in flames a few months earlier. He auditioned again, this time for a band leader in his city. The man told him to stick to driving a truck "because you're never going to make it as a singer."[2] History shows that he did, in fact, make it as a singer. More than forty years after his passing, he is still referred to as "the King of Rock 'n' Roll." Even today Elvis Presley's celebrity looms so large that he still makes more money every year than many living celebrities.

What is it that fuels the engine of celebrity culture? There is no single answer—the reasons are complex, even contradictory. We want our celebrities to be ordinary, just like the rest of us, but we also want them to be extraordinary, not like the rest of us at all. That is just one dilemma of what many refer to as the "cult of celebrity." And like any cult, it is replete with idols.

There is no question that the cult of celebrity is precisely that—it goes beyond mere interest into obsession, and often into worship.

All religions have certain similar characteristics. There is a deity, generally regarded as all-powerful, all-knowing, and omnipresent. There is a liturgy, or order of worship. There are sacred documents. There are certain locations where the deity is worshipped. There is a financial support system. There are worshippers. All of these things are present, to a greater or lesser degree, in celebrity culture. Let's explore this concept.

While celebrities are certainly not all-powerful or all-knowing, you couldn't tell that by the way their star-struck fans behave. Celebrity endorsements are sought by corporations that depend on star power to market their merchandise. From automobiles to cruises, from insurance to investments, from restaurants to resorts, celebrities auction their images and voices to the highest bidder. Their goal is to cajole and convince consumers to part with their hard-earned money. The ubiquity of these celebrity endorsements is a testimony to their effectiveness.

When it comes to being all-knowing, celebrity opinions are available through every known medium on every subject under the sun. They may not know any more about the subject they are asked to opine upon than the average twelve-year-old, but their views are magnified by their celebrity.

On the subject of omnipresence, celebrities are truly everywhere. Their countenances smile, stare, or smirk at us from billboards, television and movie screens, magazines, internet sites, and smartphones 24/7 from sea to shining sea. An entire industry has developed around those who have acquired fame. Weekly tabloids that report on celebrity culture appear on newsstands and in supermarket checkout lanes across the nation.

The liturgy of celebrity worship differs according to what type of celebrity is in focus. It might be a playlist for a music project or concert, a program for a ball game or a theater production, or an unspoken but understood ritual performed before going to a game, show, or other production.

Sacred documents of celebrity worship include any printed material, from handbills, posters, and magazine articles to transcripts from television programs, movie scripts, or books (usually authored by ghostwriters).

Venues for celebrity worship vary and range in size from a local television studio to the largest stadiums in the country. Places such as dance halls, hotel ballrooms, community theaters, and open farm fields attract adherents of the celebrity cult by the dozens or tens of thousands.

The financial support system of celebrity worship includes every kind of merchandise imaginable—and some that shouldn't be imagined. Money flows toward celebrities like water flows to the ocean. Everything that can be monetized is—including time, images, names, endorsements, autographs, opinions, costumes, artistic endeavors, creations, merchandise, and other categories too numerous to name. In addition, celebrity leads to opportunities from dignitaries and locations that would never occur absent the notoriety that celebrity affords.

Then, of course, there are the worshippers themselves. I am not suggesting that everyone who enjoys watching sporting events or who attends an occasional concert is involved in idolatry. However, it is hard to argue that the elements of worship do not profusely abound in celebrity culture. Fans number from a handful to the millions.

The term *fan* means "an enthusiastic devotee, follower, or admirer of a sport, pastime, celebrity, etc."[3] The term is a shortened version of the word *fanatic*, which means "a person with an extreme and uncritical enthusiasm or zeal, as in religion or politics."[4] The term *fanatic* comes from a Latin word that means "pertaining to a temple."[5] Just think—millions of celebrity fans label religious Americans as uncritical devotees of their preferred deity. I think the most zealous proponents of religion certainly have their match in some fans of celebrities, entertainers, sports stars, or social media mavens. This list is by no means comprehensive, but rather representative of the major streams of celebrity that overwhelmingly influence and pervade our culture. I will deal with them in order.

Ah, the cachet of celebrity! There is just nothing quite like it, in more ways than one. How else can we explain the star-studded status of some celebrities who display little to no talent yet command the attention of millions of starstruck, all-but-drooling, adoring fans?

From Zsa Zsa Gabor to Paris Hilton, the celebrity of wealthy socialites has been grist for gossip columnists for generations, with no sign of de-escalation. What any of these people actually do or create to command the attention they receive is the subject of endless debate, but the fact is that they have the attention of multitudes—at least until the next shiny new object comes along. The tabloids, the talk shows, the game shows, and the internet all ensure an audience for anyone fortunate enough to have the right physical appearance, the right amount of wealth, or the right publicists, makeup artists, consultants, and an army of others who help shovel fuel on their celebrity fire.

There are also the entertainers, those involved in film, television, theater, music, dance, comedy, and nearly every other kind of artistic endeavor (and some that are, arguably, not so artistic). The American appetite for entertainment is ferocious and insatiable despite the many thousands of people who do their best to try to satiate it.

Let's look at just one area—film, for instance. Perform the following experiment: Survey the offerings of any movie streaming service in any genre you choose. Consider the titles, look at the cover pictures, and read the summaries. Then ask yourself a few questions: How in the world do most of these movies even get approved, much less produced? It is very expensive to make a movie—where does all the money come from, and from whom? How does anyone persuade supposedly reasonable people to part with their hard-earned dollars to produce this—stuff?

I do believe that some films can legitimately be called good entertainment. I also recognize that what passes as good is a matter of personal preference. However, I also believe a consensus can be reached that a whole host of what is produced in Hollywood and elsewhere is slickly packaged and strategically promoted dreck—nothing but mind-numbing, intelligence-insulting entertainment junk food for the entertainment-aholics. This, as so many things do these days, reminds me of a story.

During a sanitation workers' strike in a major American city, people became desperate to get rid of their trash. Rubbish piled up inside and outside of homes, apartments, and office buildings. Sidewalks and streets became clogged with the detritus of a throwaway culture.

One man recognized the frequency of robberies in his city as an opportunity. He bagged up all his trash, put it in a big cardboard box, and covered the box with gift wrap, complete with ribbon and a bow. He then placed the decorated box in the back seat of his unlocked car one evening. The next morning, his "gift" was gone—thieves took out his trash free of charge.

The thieves made the same mistake that many movie watchers do: they were attracted to the packaging without bothering to ascertain the identity of the contents inside. In many cases, what is inside is not suitable for children, adults, or anyone else. Hollywood, the town that became synonymous with the movie industry in America and the world, is a study in contradictions. As with most things concerning Hollywood, separating fact from fiction is an adventure, one that generally results in questionable outcomes.

The area was first known as the Cahuenga Valley, where farmers tried with varying degrees of success to raise orchard crops. A couple who had recently relocated to Los Angeles from Kansas, Harvey and Daeida Wilcox, enjoyed the area and bought land there in 1887.

According to tradition, Daeida named it Hollywood.[6] Her husband later divided the land into tracts and sold them.

By 1902, H. J. Whitley, a land developer, arranged to have the Hollywood Hotel built to attract potential homebuyers. The town was incorporated in 1903 and merged with Los Angeles in 1910.[7]

In 1904, the residents of Hollywood voted to ban liquor except for medicinal purposes. Amazingly, movie theaters were also banned in Hollywood until the city's annexation to Los Angeles, which had no such restrictions.[8]

Moviemakers flocked to the Los Angeles area due to several factors. For one, patents held by Thomas Edison prevented the use of movie camera technology without paying royalties. Due to the distances and travel difficulties involved, patent infringements were tougher to enforce on the West Coast. If anyone did run afoul of the law, the Mexican border was only a hundred miles away. In addition, the Southern California location was adjacent to mountains, seashore, and deserts, making appealing backgrounds for motion pictures. The climate was sunny and generally agreeable, and land was cheap.[9]

By the 1920s, Hollywood was the locus of film production in America, and filmmaking was a burgeoning industry in the nation. The product the movies sold was fantasy, not reality—and Americans were buying.

One fantasy appropriated by many in the business of motion pictures is that they believe what their fans say about them. When bad behavior occurs, instead of being stopped or shamed because of it, the stars often are publicized and promoted. After all, no publicity is bad publicity when a fan base clamors for any kind of news about their chosen idol. What is a little drunk and disorderly conduct, indecent exposure, drug- or alcohol-induced fit of rage, spousal or partner abuse, serial adultery, or irrational behavior? It's all in a day's work for the inhabitants of Tinseltown.

These same behaviors and excesses apply to celebrities in other fields of entertainment, such as the music industry, but I promised to limit my remarks to movies. Let me just say that one popular television program that previews up-and-coming singers actually has the word *idol* in its title. I don't think any show could be more aptly named.

Let's leave the rest of the low-hanging fruit of entertainment and move on to another hotbed of idolatrous worship, which is college and professional sports. I say this with caution, since I live in central Ohio, where Columbus, the state capital, is home to The Ohio State University and its beloved Buckeye football team. Ohio State's athletic department sponsors thirty-six intercollegiate teams that compete every year, with revenues exceeding $250 million. Since no tuition or tax money is used to operate this self-supporting portion of the university, all that money is coming from somewhere, much of it from the pockets of fans.[10]

Despite having a mascot that regularly shows up on lists of the very worst college mascots—Brutus

Buckeye—central Ohio has more than its share of Buckeye aficionados. Many of them worship at the shrine of "the Shoe" (the informal name of Ohio Stadium, which is shaped like a very large horseshoe) for several weeks every football season. The weekly animal sacrifice is burned on barbecue grills all over the parking lots (a process known as tailgating), and prodigious quantities of sacred libations are poured out by the faithful. The same process is repeated in other stadiums by equally devout and fervent fans all across the country for several months.

If you think college football fans are radical, professional football fans likely exceed all others in terms of fanaticism. I'm talking about American football here— the kind with the ball that has pointed ends. "Football" in most of the world is "soccer" to those in the United States, and soccer fans are arguably the rowdiest and most extreme fans in the world—but I digress, since I am limiting my remarks to idolatry in America.

Fans in American football stadiums often exhibit more than just enthusiasm for a team. At times energetic support has boiled over into actual violence. Fights in the stands between fans of opposing teams (and occasionally between fans of the same team) have become so common that they don't even make headlines anymore. Many professional sports stadiums have holding cells where fans who cross the line into criminal activity can be held until the police can arrest them.[11] In fact, from 1998 to 2004, Philadelphia's Veterans Stadium had a court where a judge tried cases and sentenced unruly fans on the spot.[12]

Without a doubt many of these sports-related altercations are fueled by alcohol, which is a money machine at every stadium. But does the beer cause the bad behavior, or does the bad behavior already exist and the beer just increases the intensity? That would be a fascinating study for a sociology student searching for a topic for their master's thesis. Perhaps a jumping off point for their research may be found in Proverbs 20:1, "Wine is a mocker, strong drink is raging, and whoever is deceived by it is not wise."

Many professional athletes work extremely hard to develop their skills and display a level of proficiency that is unmatched in any other form of physical endeavor. However, I believe it is dangerous to assign athletes godlike status because of their achievements in an area that emphasizes physical attributes. This is especially true when some of these same people engage in the very worst of human behavior—such as abuse or violence, substance abuse, sexual profligacy, disrespect of all forms of authority, reckless disregard for the safety or well-being of others; the list could go on and on. Be cautious and discerning here, especially regarding your children. Remember, all human idols truly have feet of clay.

The last category I will mention is perhaps the most ubiquitous in our modern, internet-obsessed culture. They have become known as "social media influencers." I find this to be an interesting designation, considering their influence is generally not due to any achievement or proficiency in a particular area, such as science, medicine, engineering, or a trade. Their influence in most cases comes from their expertise in feeding the bottomless pit of social media users' craving for *content*. Content, in this context, is anything that is shared on a social media platform. The more views and likes a segment of content receives, the more influence the person who produces that content is said to possess.

We live in a fascinating time. The wisdom of the ages is available to us, in the form of information that has become available literally in the palms of our hands. The touch of a few buttons enables us to access a variety of viewpoints about nearly every subject under the sun, as well as quite a few that should never see the light of day. Why is it, then, that while the populace has access to the world's accumulated wisdom, they spend so much time and effort pursuing the basest and most depraved of destructive impulses?

Could it be that such content fuels the Adamic nature outside the redemptive work of the living Savior, Jesus Christ? Huh…I wonder. If not that, why do millions spend multiplied hours obsessing over where someone vacationed or what they had for lunch—or playing a game that takes them deep into a world of fantasy—or one that simply wastes their time and brain cells? First John 2:15 has this admonition, which points out the need for believers to keep themselves separate from a world that is contrary to all God is and represents: "Do not love the world or the things in the world. If anyone loves the world, the love of the Father is not in him."

What is it that gives social media influencers such influence? Is it their profound understanding of important topics, or their advanced education and experience, or their pungent distillation of complex issues, making them easy to understand? As you might guess, the answers to those questions are no, no, and no. What makes social media influencers influential is that they have enormous numbers of followers. As I have said, the more followers they acquire, the more influence they supposedly have.

The best way to understand why the goal of becoming a social media influencer is becoming so popular is to realize all that influence translates into money. The money is derived from advertisers who purchase space on the social media sites to sell their wares to those whose eyes are on that space. Additional money comes from subscriptions the influencer sells that provide access to special content or offers not available to casual visitors. The money also flows in from ideas, services, and even products that the influencers make, license, or endorse.

What is it that causes thousands, even millions of people to watch for the next content upload from their preferred internet profiteers? Most of the time it is visual stimulation in the form of videos or pictures or vlogs (a variation of *blog*, which is a shortened version of the word *weblog*). Those who do it best make the most money and thereby have the most influence. All the while, we as a culture risk sinking further into irrelevance while watching videos of other people doing stupid stuff. This idol worship can result in deadly consequences.

From time to time, so-called challenges become popular on social media. They might involve anything from dumping buckets of ice water on yourself to making yourself dizzy by running around in a circle. Some of the more outrageous ones, such as suffocating yourself until you pass out, are unusually risky. I am aware of a family whose teenage son was car surfing in a parking lot when something went wrong and he was thrown off the vehicle. The driver was unable to stop in time and ran over the boy, crushing him to death. What began as an effort to mimic behavior seen on a video ended in a heartbreaking tragedy.

Mindless obedience to or imitation of an internet influencer is a pervasive form of idolatry. It deserves no place among rational people.

# Chapter 2

# FILTERED: EGOTISM AND THE PURSUIT OF PHYSICAL PERFECTION

*Magic mirror on the wall, who is the fairest one of all?*
—THE BROTHERS GRIMM, 1812, *GRIMM'S FAIRY TALES*

*But the LORD said to Samuel, "Do not look on his appearance or on the height of his stature, because I have rejected him. For the LORD sees not as man sees. For man looks on the outward appearance, but the LORD looks on the heart."*
—1 SAMUEL 16:7

OF ALL THE attributes that are accorded to humanity, the one that may be the most subjective, not to mention the most fleeting, is beauty. Proverbs 31:30 says, "Charm is deceitful, and beauty is vain." This same phenomenon is found throughout the natural world. Flowers are beautiful, but they are fragile and last for only a few days. Monarch butterflies are beautiful, but their life spans are only two weeks to nine months. A sunset or moonrise may be beautiful, but it changes in a moment, and if you miss the moment, you may also miss the beauty.

There is an infinite range of physical characteristics that may be considered beautiful, and that will change based solely upon who is judging. There is no single universal standard concerning what constitutes beauty. Nonetheless, this is belied by current trends in various domains across America. Regarding fashion, form, and features, there are many forces that attempt, at times successfully, to require conformity to an artificial standard as the norm.

Let's take reputed "beauty" pageants as an example. Although I'll admit it's been many years since I have witnessed one, the most remarkable thing that struck me was how all the young ladies in the pageant looked. With few exceptions, they were essentially the same. Although some were taller or a bit shorter, some had dark hair while others had light hair, and they appeared in a variety of outfits, the women were essentially alike. Conformity to a certain standard was quite obviously the rule. The question I had then and still have now is this: What wise and highly exalted person or persons decide what the standard should be?

Certainly, God is a God of endless variety. Have you ever examined a flake of snow? No two are alike, and all are exquisitely beautiful. That which appeals to one person, people group, or culture may not be attractive to another.

During the Victorian era—and even later in Europe and elsewhere—the standard to which many women sought to conform was having the illusion of a tiny waist. The corset, an undergarment that constricted a lady's waist and, in extreme cases (tightlacing), restricted her movement, was all the rage. Women also wore other garments that, when combined with their corseted middle, gave the impression of a small waist (the so-called hourglass figure). Corsets were reinforced with whalebone, reeds, or even steel.

In China, for generations a practice was used that gives new meaning to the expression "beauty is pain," ladies: the custom of foot binding. The idea was that tiny feet (in women) were fashionable. To conform, ladies would go to excruciating extremes to physically confine the natural growth of their feet, including breaking their toes and deforming their bones to achieve this standard. Pain, infection, and restricted movement were the most common results, yet remarkably the practice persisted for hundreds of years.

For thousands of years there have existed certain people groups in Africa and Asia who believe that neck rings are fashionable, and many women in those groups wear them from the time they are very young. Such rings are a sign of wealth. Rings also give the appearance of a long neck, which is a symbol of beauty preferred in those cultures.

I don't know of any equivalent practices in

twenty-first-century America, but I have observed some trends over the years that are apparently adhered to for aesthetics rather than any other consideration such as comfort.

High-heeled shoes are one example. Once the exclusive domain of royalty (especially men), high heels have long been a symbol of high fashion. Functionality is another matter. Anyone who has ever seen a video of models collapsing on the catwalk while attempting to strut along in their stilettos can attest that following certain fashion trends involves considerable risk.

Another example with which I do have limited personal experience is eyebrow tweezing. Now, before you raise your eyebrow in surprise at such an admission, let me explain.

The old adage asserts, "Love is blind, and marriage is an eye-opener." After Joni and I were married, I arose one morning to an unfamiliar sight—there was a woman in my bathroom. (It was my wife.) She was leaning over the vanity, looking intently into the mirror and holding something akin to a surgical instrument in her hand while making motions to which I was not accustomed.

"What are you doing?" I asked.

"I'm plucking my eyebrows," Joni responded.

I was intrigued. "Does it hurt?" I inquired.

She gazed at me with the inimitable expression pulled by wives the world over when they realize they need to explain something to a clueless husband.

"Silly boy," she said. "No, it doesn't hurt." She turned

her attention to the mirror again and then said, "By the way, it wouldn't hurt you to try this. You're supposed to have two eyebrows, not just one."

I tried very hard to keep the indignation out of my voice as I replied, "Let me try it." Joni handed me the tweezers. I thought it would be more efficient to pluck out a bunch of hairs at a time rather than only one, so I grasped a tuft. I may have flexed my bicep for effect. I clamped the tweezers tightly between my fingers and gave a mighty jerk.

Several things happened in immediate succession. It felt as though every one of those eyebrow hairs had roots that went all the way down to my toenails. Somewhere from deep within my soul a high-pitched shriek escaped me. I threw the tweezers into the sink and exclaimed, "Good heavens, woman! Don't ever touch those again!"

This illustrates what social critics and commentators have been saying for years—there is an unfair and unrighteous double standard in place in many cultures regarding the physical appearances of men and women. Women are expected to achieve and maintain a certain standard of beauty. Men, on the other hand, can look however they please without much stigma being attached to them. There are two areas where this is most pronounced in America.

One is the entertainment industry. In movies or any other visual media, women, regardless of their age, are required to look "good," however that may be defined. "Good" usually implies unblemished skin, bright eyes, no wrinkles, no sags, no extra pounds, and full hair, as well as fashionable clothes, shoes, and accessories. It may take a lot of time or expense to achieve this look, especially as the years go by, but the idol of beauty must be appeased.

Men, on the other hand, are permitted to be a bit paunchy, raunchy, bearded, unkempt, balding, and graying, with more wrinkles than a box of prunes. They can fall out of bed, pull a comb through whatever hair they have left, and still not be referred to pejoratively as "past their prime" or "over the hill." Rather, they are designated as "distinguished" looking.

According to one study, women's earnings in film peaked at age thirty-four and then dropped precipitously. Men's earning potential in film, on the other hand, didn't peak until age fifty-one, and in many cases these men kept earning until they retired or died.[1] Although changes have been made, there is still a discrepancy in the film industry between men and women of similar ages.

The other area where idolatry requires more of women than of men is the area of cosmetics, a centuries-old concept that has become a multibillion-dollar industry worldwide. The ancient Egyptians were renowned for popularizing cosmetics, especially eye shadow, eyeliner, face powder, and lipstick. Both men and women, especially of the upper classes, used makeup regularly. Some researchers suspect that the black eyeliner so prevalent in ancient Egyptian illustrations had the practical effect of protecting the eyes from the sun's glare as well as being considered attractive.

Ancient cultures the world over had their own makeup traditions, including China, Japan, India, Mesopotamia, Greece, and Rome. In every case the predominant users of makeup were women.

In America, cosmetics has a long and varied history with wide extremes of popularity. For most of the nineteenth century, makeup was associated with sordid occupations and seedy classes. Most respectable women avoided it. Beginning with the rise of the popularity of films in the 1920s, people began to accept the idea of women wearing makeup, and the industry burgeoned. World War II accelerated its acceptance. Different styles predominated in successive decades, but makeup is here to stay. One development is the so-called natural look, which ironically takes a lot of time and effort to accomplish. A well-known and highly respected country music artist known for her use of cosmetics quipped jokingly, "It costs a lot of money to look this cheap"![2]

There is no telling why a certain trend will predominate. In years gone by it was considered fashionable for women to have pale skin, since only the lower classes worked outdoors and were exposed to the sun. Many years later, pale skin became regarded as unhealthy looking. The only solution was to go to the beach or pool on a sunny day and lie on a towel while slathering one's body with lotion and risking sunburn and skin cancer. More recently, people paid to roast themselves in tanning beds to achieve the desired tone to their skin.

In addition to the cosmetics industry, the fashion industry is a significant driver of the cult of personal appearance. I say "industry" because it is big business worldwide, valued at $1.7 trillion in 2022.[3]

I don't suppose it would be inaccurate to say the fashion industry began when Adam and his wife covered themselves with leaves in an attempt to hide their shame in Genesis 3. God provided a more permanent solution with the garments of animal skins that He gave them, which was the first use of leather or fur as clothing.

For millennia ordinary people had only such articles of clothing that were absolutely necessary to protect them from exposure to the elements or to serve some other utilitarian purpose. In ancient times, in some cultures, to be unclothed was reserved for children or slaves. Only those who had wealth or power wore clothing indicating their high social status. Now, clothing is used more as an expression of individuality, status, or wealth than for any other purpose.

Remember the words of the Lord Jesus in Matthew 6:21 (KJV): "For where your treasure is, there will your heart be also." You could say your spending reflects your idolatry. Consider that Americans spend more money per capita on clothing and shoes than any other nation on earth—$819.[4] That money purchased 17 billion units of apparel, most of which will end up in a landfill within a short time.[5] Environmentalists regret this development, especially since natural materials such as wool or cotton cloth are easily recyclable. Unfortunately, polyester, which is made from oil and is an increasingly common ingredient in clothing, is not.

But wait—I thought Hollywood, politicians, and the wealthy were concerned about the environment!

When I was young, my family recycled clothing all the time. When a garment had outlived its purpose, we would never simply throw it away until it had achieved successive seasons of usefulness—first as clothing for the next child in line and then as a quite-useful shop or cleaning rag.

Recently, clothing has gone from durable to disposable. On average, people wear an article of clothing only seven times. The average consumer purchases 60 percent more clothing today than in the year 2000, and we wear 60 percent of our clothes for less than a year.[6]

These factors have little, if anything, to do with need. They are driven by the idols of fashion trends, conformity, and personal appearance. If we don't look a certain way, we don't feel approval from others. If we don't feel approval from others, we don't feel good about ourselves. If we don't feel good about ourselves, we tend to do something to change that; in America, this often involves buying something. The fashion industry is more than happy to accommodate and help fuel the obsession.

When fashion won't do the trick and cosmetic lotions and potions aren't enough, there is always the fitness industry. Here again, before we proceed, a reminder from page one of this chapter: "For man looks on the outward appearance, but the LORD looks on the heart" (1 Sam. 16:7). Once again, I use the term *industry* here because there are around 32,000 fitness centers in the US, generating about $30 billion in yearly revenue.[7]

Many people pay a monthly fee to access the gym's exercise equipment. Statistics show that 50 percent of new gym members typically quit within the first six months,[8] and 67 percent of gym memberships go completely unused.[9] What a business—sell a membership, keep the money, and 67 percent of your members will never use the facility! I think I'll look for a franchise.

A typical gym may have several thousand members but be able to accommodate at most a few hundred of them at any given time. In other words, the gym is depending on you to not show up, and they are not disappointed when you don't.

Even if you are faithful to attend the gym regularly, you will probably never end up looking like the fitness models you see on the covers of magazines—that would require a special measure of devotion that a minuscule number of people are willing to make. However, the beautiful folks pictured on magazine covers usually don't look like that either—photographic manipulation can do wonders, and it is not a recent development. Even in the Victorian era some studios could alter photographs to accentuate certain features.

If you graduated from high school in the same era in which I did, you probably dreaded seeing proofs of your senior pictures with all the blemishes you knew you had on picture day. You may recall the relief you felt when you noticed they were gone in the final picture that was used in your high school yearbook. The photography studio had worked its magic.

Advances in technology provide new and more effective tools for photograph alteration. People can post pictures that make themselves look like anyone—and sometimes they do. Instead of real people, what we actually see amounts to avatars. Can you imagine the following absurdity? A person posts their "picture" on social media. They have darkened their hair, erased their wrinkles, changed their eye color, tightened up their neck skin, and improved their appearance in countless ways. Then they share a message announcing their desire for an authentic relationship! Truth in advertising does not apply. The idol of appearance must be satisfied at all costs.

Our culture has yet another cure for all those who desire to improve their physical appearance. Weight-loss clinics, diet plans, specialty cookbooks, and medical procedures are readily available and promise breathtaking improvements. The image idol offers a host of pledges and assurances, most of which are extremely exaggerated—or blatantly untrue.

Once again, we live in an age and among a culture of vast contradictions. We are offered greater conveniences and more choices regarding food than any previous generation, yet we are more unhealthy than ever. Diabetes, high blood pressure, heart disease, and other ailments are in many cases the high cost of our lifestyles. Forty-five million Americans begin a diet program every year.[10] In fact, the diet and weight-loss industry generates $71 billion each year.[11] The sad reality is that, depending on what literature you read, between 65 and 95 percent of diets fail.[12]

For the most impassioned of worshippers at the shrine of image idolatry there are always cosmetic procedures, both surgical and nonsurgical. Together they amounted to $11.8 billion in 2022.[13]

In 2019, before the COVID-19 pandemic reduced the number of procedures in 2020, the top five plastic surgeries performed in the US were as follows:

1. Rhinoplasty (nose reshaping)—over 362,000

2. Blepharoplasty (eyelid surgery)—over 354,000

3. Augmentation mammaplasty (breast augmentation)—over 287,000

4. Liposuction—over 265,000

5. Rhytidectomy (facelift)—over 261,000[14]

That amounts to more than 1.5 million procedures in one year. The idol of appearance obviously has an enormous appetite, and millions of devotees are compulsively eager to satisfy its ceaseless cravings. People puff it up, paint it in, and powder it over, and if all of that doesn't satisfy the beast, they pull it out, cut it off, and sew it back. In the words of comedian Joan Rivers, "I've had so much plastic surgery, when I die they will donate my body to Tupperware."[15]

Let's keep in mind that plastic surgery will never

make anyone younger. According to Job 14:5, a person's days on earth are determined by God. Even his months are under heaven's control. Man has been given only an allotted time. Remember, the death rate among humans remains stubbornly at 100 percent.

The living God created us with the gift of eyesight. It is perhaps the most valuable and useful of our physical senses. It provides us with a mechanism to receive information about and make sense of the world around us. It is therefore no surprise that we have tremendous reliance upon what we see. However, we must never forget the Lord Jesus' admonition in John 7:24: "Do not judge according to appearance, but practice righteous judgment."

When you are trying to cross the street, by all means use your eyes and believe what they tell you, and make decisions accordingly. Keep in mind that those types of decisions relate to the natural world. But know this: when it comes to your spiritual life, you cannot depend solely upon the information delivered to your brain by your physical senses. The world is satiated with deception.

Jesus plainly told us the nature of the devil and his kingdom in John 8:44: "When he lies, he speaks from his own nature, for he is a liar and the father of lies." The enemy of your soul would like nothing better than for you to make eternal decisions based on temporal information. Keep that in mind the next time you are tempted to judge someone's character by their outward appearance. Second Corinthians 4:18 is instructive:

"While we do not look at the things which are seen, but at the things which are not seen. For the things which are seen are temporal, but the things which are not seen are eternal."

As you have probably discovered by this point in your life, the god of self is a cruel taskmaster. It promises fulfillment and produces failure. Selfishness leads to death. Selflessness leads to life. Jesus said so in Matthew 10:39: "He who finds his life will lose it, and he who loses his life for My sake will find it."

In Greek mythology, Narcissus was a young man who was unblemished and unusually beautiful from birth. As he grew beyond adolescence, he spurned those who sought his affection. Eventually he saw his own reflection in a pool of water and fell in love with it. He died (some versions of the myth say he committed suicide) because he could not possess the object of his obsessive self-love.

Narcissism is a personality style related to self-esteem. Everyone has it to some degree, since we should all have a healthy yet realistic determination of our self-worth. However, some people possess an idolatrous and dangerous degree of narcissism, which is called narcissistic personality disorder. Those plagued by this condition generally have some or all of the following characteristics:

◊ A sense of entitlement

◊ Manipulative behavior

◊ A constant need for admiration

◊ Lack of empathy

◊ Arrogance[16]

So, where does this leave us with regard to the idol of self? I am not suggesting that if you indulge in a bowl of ice cream or a piece of chocolate from time to time you are in danger of making yourself into an idol. I am saying the tendency to think only in terms of "me, myself, and I" is reaching critical mass in America and is characteristic of the damaging and damning cult of self. The biblical directive remains clear: "For I say, through the grace given to me, to everyone among you, not to think of himself more highly than he ought to think, but to think with sound judgment, according to the measure of faith God has distributed to every man" (Rom. 12:3).

The apostle Paul's teaching in 1 Corinthians 11:31 is deeply valuable: "If we would judge ourselves, we would not be judged." Humility, self-reflection, and self-evaluation are necessary tools to help us understand who we are and where we fit in the world. However, if the majority of a person's thinking is focused inward and they rarely, if ever, consider others, that person is in deep danger of becoming a worshipper of one of the most subtle and destructive idols known to fallen man— the idol of self.

## Chapter 3

# INSATIABLE: THE RACE FOR POWER, INFLUENCE, AND STATUS

*Power tends to corrupt, and absolute power corrupts absolutely.*
—JOHN DALBERG-ACTON, 1887

*For they loved the praise of men more than the praise of God.*
—JOHN 12:43

**M**Y FATHER RAISED me to "never get above my raisin'." He told me those who "wore a big hat but had no cattle" were the epitome of arrogance. Another saying that people from my ancestral home in eastern Kentucky use when they perceive someone to have acquired an inflated sense of their own importance is, "They've become too big for their britches." (In this context *britches* is a colloquial pronunciation of *breeches*, also known as trousers.)

A casual assessment of our culture reveals there are plenty of people who have outgrown their figurative pants—and for those who would accuse me of engaging in fat-shaming, this observation has nothing to do with anyone's physical dimensions. I suppose the most obvious segment of this category would be professional politicians and bureaucrats. It is almost too easy to target many of our elected officials—and others who were not elected but appointed—as the poster children for runaway egos, industrial-strength self-aggrandizement, and shameless hypocrisy. Blatant lies and manipulative distortions of truth flow from their ridiculous rhetoric and thoughtless talking points in much the same way that water spills over the falls of Niagara. There are several reasons they attempt such deception with alarming alacrity.

One deeply insulting reason is their faux intellectual superiority. They count on enough of the electorate having low IQs and being uninformed voters. Therefore, they have no fear that they will ever be questioned or challenged about anything they say.

Another reason functioning in tandem with the first is that they realize the American press is no longer interested in reporting factual truth without party bias. The great divide is well established. Party politics is the driving force as news outlets have become nothing more than an arm of one of the two major political parties, never asking hard questions or presenting alternative scenarios to the agendas they are promoting.

Special interest groups are another factor. They

pressure and persuade politicians to act in ways that defy common sense and certainly in no way protect the common good. The politician is expected to carry water for a particular industry, business, faction, or economic sector to gain some advantage while the special interest group supplies the millions of dollars needed to get them elected in the first place.

Yet another boost to these individuals' gargantuan egos comes from constantly being asked their opinions, put in front of video cameras, and having their statements quoted in the media. The more face time or print space they gain, or the more times their name is mentioned, the greater their influence over the unthinking, undiscerning masses becomes.

Finally, career politicians have a built-in survival instinct. They know that the most lucrative rewards come based on continued time in office, so they do whatever they need to do and say whatever they need to say to continue being reelected or reappointed. Once they manage to plant themselves in a seat on the gravy train, it becomes increasingly difficult for them to get off.

It is no secret that politicians at every level are subjected to offers of favors, special consideration, and cold, hard cash in return for special treatment of whomever is offering them the perquisites. Do they ever accept these offers? One man was quoted as saying you could "buy a senator" for as little as $10,000.[1]

Obviously the money will keep coming only if the official remains in their position. Of course their ability to serve as an independent decision maker who conscientiously represents their constituents will be compromised, but that's just the way this idolatrous game is played. The appearance of impropriety is of no consequence to these exalted lawmakers, who continue to be reelected and all but enshrined as objects of worship regardless of how apparent it is to the casual observer that their public service is only enriching them personally. In contrast, observe what Proverbs 17:23 (MSG) says: "The wicked take bribes under the table; they show nothing but contempt for justice."

For the majority of officials, being elected to multiple terms has become the rule rather than the exception. Name recognition is the most compelling factor voters rely on when presented with options on a ballot, so someone who is already in office naturally has the advantage. Incumbency also brings the advantage of a politician already being in a position to help their constituents rather than only promising to do so as a challenger.

Campaigns have become big business in their own right, and it seems as though anyone seeking office must be more adept at fundraising than they are at finding solutions for problems or coherently addressing issues. In the case of unelected officials, they often find a way to burrow into the burgeoning bureaucracy and become insulated from even the suggestion of ideas different from their own.

Term limits have some positive effect against the ills presented by career politicians. However, even in cases in which term limits have been declared constitutional, those who are term limited from one office often simply run for another office and thereby remain politicians in perpetuity.

Not only are politicians worshipped at the shrine of power, but people also defend their preferred politicians regardless of how ungodly, reckless, irresponsible, or corrupt they become. In a representative republic such as ours, individual citizens have a responsibility to reward those who are doing a good job and restrict those who are not. In other words, it's on us!

The majority of Americans don't tune in to political issues every day. They want to be left alone to live their private lives as they choose. As a result, they are unaware of the misadventures of government officials— and when they do hear about them, they often find themselves bewildered by the sheer volume of misinformation that is magnified by the legacy media. (I will have more to say about that shortly.)

The unrestrained entitlement among government officials is overwhelming. During the height of the recent pandemic, one legislator appeared on national television and proudly displayed a trove of ice cream in an upscale freezer in her home.[2] Others scold common people for using fossil fuels to run home appliances as they themselves jet off to exotic vacation or conference destinations.[3] Still others are serial fabulists, embellishing their personal histories and claiming honors they did not earn.[4] The list goes on indefinitely. Here is an admonition from Proverbs 16:18 that is nearly universally ignored but is universally true: "Pride goes before destruction, and a haughty spirit before a fall."

Of course, among the political class there are always the good old-fashioned liars, who do so glibly and repeatedly with no sense of shame. They lie so often that it becomes an ingrained habit, and with the confidence that only comes from knowing that nobody with any kind of access to them will challenge the validity of their claims. When anyone has the temerity to mention conditions that contradict their lies, they invent another lie that is usually even more outrageous than the previous one. When there is nothing to lie about, they make something up, even though telling the truth would be easier. It would be a pathetic scenario if such individuals were not positioned on idolatrous pedestals of power—but since they are, it is downright dangerous.

Consider this quote from President James A. Garfield: "Now, more than ever before, the people are responsible for the character of their Congress. If that body be ignorant, reckless, and corrupt, it is because the people tolerate ignorance, recklessness, and corruption. If it be intelligent, brave, and pure, it is because the people demand these high qualities to represent them in the national legislature....If the next centennial does not find us a great nation...it will be because those who represent the enterprise, the culture, and the morality of the nation do not aid in controlling the political forces."[5]

Garfield was assassinated in 1881 after serving only six months in the White House. His comments are more timely now than when he uttered them. Here is another, from a speech Garfield gave in 1865: "A government which does not draw its inspiration of liberty, justice, and morality from the people will soon become both tyrannical and corrupt."[6] Garfield may have never claimed the mantle of a prophet, but it seems his words were more prophetic than those spoken by many who call themselves by that title.

To the category of individuals who are prone to worshipping at the shrine of power, I add the media. First, let me clarify what I mean by the term *media*. In days gone by, newspapers dominated the business of factual information sharing. It would be hard to convince people today of the influence that newspapers had on communities even fifty years ago. Nearly everyone who could read looked to the newspaper to inform them regarding events and issues. In many places, more than one paper could be found, and in larger cities several dailies were available. Newspaper headlines became the grist of conversations throughout the marketplace.

As technology proliferated, other forms of communication competed with and eventually supplanted newspapers as major sources of information. Telegraph lines sprouted across the country, providing a means of nearly instantaneous communication. Later, radio rapidly developed into a wellspring of news as well as entertainment. Then radio's younger sibling, television, became nearly universal as a means of communicating information and providing amusement.

Each of these was only a prelude to the plethora of media outlets that are available today and in ways that could not have been imagined by the newspaper magnates of past generations. Virtually anyone, anywhere can now gather and disseminate information, a development that provides great opportunity but also great danger, which I will discuss elsewhere.

When I was young, newspapers were still popular and expanding. Most of them were just as their name implied—filled with news. It may have been local, national, or even international news, but it was mostly news that they published. Editorial opinion was limited to the editorial page. Some papers carried regular editorial features by columnists who became quite well known. I remember hearing folks quote their favorite columnist with the same certainty with which some people quoted the Bible.

In many ways, radio built upon the success of newspapers in that regard. Some radio commentators became household names with programs that aired at the same time every weekday and gained a multitude of listeners who repeated what they heard on the radio as incontrovertibly true.

Television parlayed the advantages of radio exponentially because the medium was not only audible but visual as well. Those who narrated the news became instantly famous, not because they possessed any specific area of expertise but because they became adept at reading news reports in a believable way. Gathering around the television to watch the evening news became nearly a ritualistic act of devotion and worship in America, as stories were told and retold. A few national television networks were competing for the same viewership, so news anchors were compelled to appeal to as broad a swath of demographics as possible.

As with newspapers, television provided editorial comment, which was clearly identified as such. For the most part viewers trusted the networks to provide unbiased information reliably and truthfully. It was hard for most people to fathom that carefully coiffed and perfectly polished newsmen (and later, newswomen) who came into your home every evening, looked you in the eye, and communicated their pronouncements with such certainty would ever tell you anything but the truth. So, the populace assumed, "They wouldn't put it on television if it wasn't true, would they?" My, my—how times change!

Media organizations fulfilled another important function: they could be relied upon to ask difficult questions of the people in power so that any dishonesty or fraudulent activity would be identified and exposed. They were credited with being the guardians of liberties that may have been infringed upon by those in government, industry, or business.

As time passed and technology continued to develop, electronically mediated communication was thrust to the forefront. Email became a quick and convenient method of sharing information. Cell phones became more affordable and more available. Texting now takes the place of voice communication in most cases. Video uploads are an even newer method of sharing information. Multiplied millions now host blogs, webcasts, and YouTube channels; therefore, everyone is a potential journalist, and the monopoly that media corporations once held on news has become a thing of the past.

These innovations occur parallel to other developments. Traditional media outlets tend to blur the line between opinion and news to the point that no clear distinction can be made between them. As a result, some media outlets have become nothing more than mouthpieces for particular points of view. Today, rather than challenging the agendas of government officials, corporate officers, educators, industry leaders, or purveyors of new social and sexual constructs, the media often merely amplifies the talking points of those they should be questioning.

Have you ever seen the media report information that directly contradicted what you were seeing with your own eyes? One of the most startling examples is reporters presenting video footage of burning buildings while maintaining that the protests they are covering are "fiery but mostly peaceful" or "not, generally speaking, unruly."[7] I suppose if a demonstration is mostly peaceful, that means it is partly violent.

Good communicators know that for their message to be most effective, what people see should actually line up with what they hear. If it doesn't, it is a mixed message at best. People are far more likely to believe what they see than the words someone else uses to describe the scene. As cases like these continue to occur, the media's credibility will and should continue to crater.

Power is defined as "possession of control, authority, or influence over others."[8] It seems that many in the legacy media have clearly abandoned their traditional roles of impartial news gatherers and have become advocates of specific agendas. Their purpose is apparent: to influence the opinions of news consumers. One undoubtedly unintended consequence has been a deep and broadening mistrust of the media. A recent survey indicates that the majority of Americans not only no longer trust the media, but they also believe the media intends to mislead them.[9]

Social media involves an entirely different height, depth, width, and breadth of idolatrous indulgence. When it comes to influence, suffice it to say here that the owners of the largest social media platforms are often referred to as the "masters of the universe."[10] They have been accused—and exposed—of amplifying certain points of view and censoring others.

When news consumers hear something over and over again, repeated on different platforms and in different ways, they have a natural tendency to believe it. When other stories are given little or no attention, or when they are identified as misinformation, the ordinary news consumer tends to give them little regard, even if the stories are factual. The attitude is, "I believe what I heard, so don't confuse me with the facts." In this way, the influence of the social media outlets grows stronger every day, with hundreds of millions worshipping with their fingers on the keyboards or screens. It is little wonder that these outlets vehemently resist any discussion regarding their regulation or control.

Misinformation is not a new development. A quote that has famously been misattributed to Mark Twain is, "If you don't read the newspaper you are uninformed. If you do read the newspaper you are misinformed." Interesting, isn't it, that the attribution of the authorship of this quote about misinformation is itself misinformation, since there is no evidence that Twain ever said this—although I am sure he would have if he had thought of it.

Another type of power worshipper is those who need to move about in the right social circles, attend the right events, and associate with the right people—"right," of course, meaning those who have attained a certain level of prominence or status. A premier opportunity for such interaction is the Met Gala, known as the world's most prestigious and exclusive fashion event. It was described by Parade.com as "attended only by the glitziest A-list celebrities."[11] Held nearly every year since 1948, it is a fundraising event for the Metropolitan Museum of Art's Costume Institute in New York City. The guest list is limited to six hundred people, and an invitation is one of the most coveted in social circles. Tickets for the 2023 affair allegedly cost $50,000 each.[12]

Guests of the Met Gala are expected to dress according to the theme for that year's event. Most themes require haute couture and custom-made attire—to say that these garments are expensive would be like saying hell is hot. Nevertheless, those who score an invitation can say they have rubbed shoulders with the most well-bred or most well-fed, or both, in the upper echelons of high society. Just being seen there can contribute immeasurably to someone's reputation or bottom line. Of course, for those for whom that is most important, it can be a career-making opportunity.

The Met Gala is not the only event that features power, prestige, and prominence, though. Awards ceremonies of all kinds are also replete with those who want to be seen with and by all the right people. In the case of the Academy Awards ceremony, the "right" people are involved in the movie industry. Just being nominated to win a gold-plated statuette of a naked man holding a sword and standing on a five-spoked film reel is considered by some to be an honor more cherished than life itself. And oh, how the nominees and winners bask in the unmitigated idol worship of the commoners.

It seems as though entertainment in every form has its own award program: the Grammys for the music industry, the Tonys for Broadway theater productions, and the Emmys for television performances. Being nominated for any of them is regarded as an honor. Incredibly, eighteen people have won all four—known as an EGOT (for Emmy, Grammy, Oscar, and Tony).

The final category of status seekers I want to direct your attention toward comprises those who inhabit the hallowed halls of academia. There is no doubt a certain amount of academic rigor required to obtain a PhD or similar degree. The reading requirements alone are daunting, as well they should be.

I have found that in some cases those who have achieved an advanced degree consider themselves—and are considered by others—to be automatic experts in everything. When they are asked questions about areas in which they are certainly not experts, their opinions are still treated as gospel truth simply because they have a certain designation after their name. The same is true of the aforementioned category. It's almost an out-of-body experience to watch an actor who three months ago was waiting tables in New York City be asked questions or offer up their opinions on the most perplexing problems of humanity, as if a role on a sitcom or reality show somehow qualifies them to speak about global affairs. Proverbs 14:3 says, "Proud fools talk too much" (GNT).

I have encountered more than a few people with advanced degrees who could not write a coherent letter. Their musings about matters outside their field of study are usually no more reliable than anyone else's. Within disciplines such as economics, history, or language arts there are specialties that require much time and effort to master. Attention to one area of specialty may preclude becoming an expert in another. Even when people are well aware of their limitations, it is difficult to resist the temptation to offer an opinion on a matter about which they are in no regard proficient. It can be especially difficult when microphones and television cameras are thrust into their faces.

As I often say, never allow a university professor to stroke his long goatee, lean back in his leather chair, puff on his pipe and release a wreath of smoke to encircle his head like a crown, and intimidate you with his professed intellectual superiority. Always keep this in mind: for everyone who graduated at the top of his or her class, someone else graduated at the bottom. As the old joke says, "Do you know what they call the person who graduated last in their class at medical school? A doctor!"

Those who seek power, influence, or status comprise a surprising percentage of our wayward culture. Those three things make terrible idols, as do the people who pursue them to the exclusion of all else.

# Chapter 4

# STAGNANT STREAMS: ROUTINE RELIGION

*You don't get rich writing science fiction. If you want to get rich, you start a religion.*
—L. RON HUBBARD, 1948

*I hate, I despise your festivals, and I am not pleased by your solemn assemblies.*
—AMOS 5:21

WOULD IT SURPRISE you to know that there is no scholarly consensus on what constitutes a religion? You can find a definition of the word in any dictionary, but what religion actually means differs depending on what authority you consult.

Most textbook definitions of the term *religion* include concepts such as acknowledgement of a God or gods;

the existence of the supernatural; and certain beliefs, practices, rites, and rituals.

Ancient cultures the world over did not historically have a concept of religion that was separate or distinct from their usual routines or manner of living. Many ancient languages had no word that could be explicitly translated "religion." Their beliefs and practices were simply fundamental to how they lived as individuals, communities, or nations. Apparently these cultures had neither the need nor the desire to distinguish their method of worship from their manner of daily living.

Some scholars believe the term *religion* was popularized with the rise of Western Christianity. It is interesting to note that Western culture is also perhaps the most insistent that religion be a totally separate component of one's life rather than a vital element of an integrated lifestyle. Such an existence is entirely antithetical to authentic Christianity, as well as contradictory to a thoroughly biblical worldview.

It is instructive to recognize Christianity as a belief system in order to distinguish it from other religions. Today there are four major religions in our world that represent approximately 92 percent of the world's population: Christianity, Islam, Hinduism, and Buddhism. In addition, there may be as many as ten thousand religions worldwide, most of them limited to a region, culture, or people group.[1]

Contributing to further uncertainty is the proclivity of some religions to be syncretistic—that is, they combine elements of different religions into their own system of belief or practice. When this occurs, adherents often object and respond with a reform movement that attempts to return to a more fundamental understanding of what the original religion represented. Such a reform movement often becomes a religion itself.

Confused yet? Wait, there is more! Every religion has suffered schism and division. Within Christianity there are Catholics and Protestants, with the Eastern branch of Christianity (the Eastern Orthodox church and others) not to be forgotten. Protestant Christianity itself is divided into multiple denominations, such as Episcopalians, Presbyterians, Baptists, Methodists, Pentecostals, and many others.

In addition, there are other groups that claim to be Christian and utilize the language of Christianity, but they fail to pass the test of orthodoxy in several important respects. Quasi-Christian groups regard other texts to be equally important and reliable as the Bible (they are not). Some sects exalt their founders or leaders to the status of infallibility (again, they are not), or claim that they alone are the custodians of truth, and anyone who believes any other doctrine is doomed.

Perhaps of even greater importance, every group that claims to be Christian but is actually a cult invariably exhibits a defective and unscriptural view of the Lord Jesus Christ. They won't disclose their false beliefs when they come knocking on your door, but if you take the time to examine what they believe—and you must—these deficiencies and others will manifest in short order.

False doctrine has been around as long as people

have preached the gospel. Second Peter 2:1 says, "But there were also false prophets among the people, just as there will be false teachers among you, who will secretly bring in destructive heresies, even denying the Lord who bought them, bringing swift destruction upon themselves."

The current "anti-God" culture has made it fashionable to be critical of Christianity for its followers' seeming inability to agree about anything. However, splits and splinters are by no means limited to those who claim to be Christians. The largest distinction in Islam is between Sunni and Shia, with other, smaller schools of thought such as Salafism and Wahhabism also attracting attention. Denominations within Hinduism include Vaishnavism, Shaivism, Shaktism, and others. In Buddhism we find Theravada Buddhism, Mahayana Buddhism, Vajrayana Buddhism, and more.

I mention this because those who are only familiar with Christianity point to the divisions they see among those of the Christian faith. They often overlook or are ignorant of the division and dissension that exists among those loyal to other religions. Christianity is by no means unique in its followers' inability to get along with each other. That is a condition of humanity, not a characteristic that distinguishes one religion to the exclusion of the others.

Christianity has also fallen prey to criticism as a result of so many who call themselves followers of Christ yet live as strangers to the character of the One they claim to serve. These idolatrous worshippers are Christians in name only and not in practice. If such a person were placed in a lineup with any number of worshippers of other idols, they would not be distinguishable from the others.

A meme that has circulated for many years goes like this: If you were arrested and tried in a court of law for being a Christian, would there be enough evidence to convict you? I have two observations about that. First, many individuals accused of being Christians would be quickly acquitted of all charges. And second, the day may be soon at hand when true believers will be accused, arrested, and tried for crimes against the state and their fellow man when their only true "crimes" are fully surrendering their lives to the lordship of Jesus Christ and attempting to live out their convictions.

Are there Buddhists in name only? Hindus? Muslims? I have no doubt there are. Insincerity is not limited to Christianity. There will always be those who are devout in the practice of their religion and others who are luke-warm. Still others will be cold, regardless of the religion with which they choose to affiliate themselves.

I believe that many in the modern Christian church—which is quite different from the church in which I was raised and spent the first twenty-five years of my gospel ministry—remain cold-hearted in their backslidden and carnal condition because of the leaders with whom they identify.

The pastors under whose preaching I sat for many years were men of some limitations, as all men are. However, they understood and internalized that Jesus Christ was the only means of salvation, and they were never afraid to say so clearly and forcefully. They held the line of holiness against the onslaught of popular opinion and popular culture. They were fearless warriors for true, biblical morality. They were as honest and upright in their personal lives outside of the pulpit as when they were preaching from the pulpit—and everyone in the church and the community were convinced of it. They were rightly respected and held in high esteem as representatives of God Almighty.

How different conditions are today. Men such as I just described would not only be anomalies, they would be outliers in a majority of pulpits today. Yesterday's preachers thundered sermons about sin, repentance, and judgment—a far and sad cry from today's who test the winds of political correctness, and who fear cancel culture but not their Creator's counsel. These simper and snivel about felt needs, shared experiences, and unique journeys.

Yesterday's preacher called sinners to repentance. Today's pulpiteers refuse to even acknowledge sin, so there is no need to call anyone to anything, except to understand someone's struggle. They strive, above all, to be tolerant and inclusive. Yesterday's preachers denounced homosexuality and all of its demonic derivatives as the abominations they are. Today, homosexuals have exited the closet and entered the pulpit. Modern church leaders of entire denominations have embraced what the founders of those same denominations rejected. Man is magnified above his Maker, sin is celebrated, and sanctification is sacrificed on the idolatrous altar of self.

Yesterday's preachers made do with 40-watt light bulbs hung from the ceiling on single wires. Today we have light shows and special effects that would make rock stars from the '90s envious. In the past, preachers affirmed they would follow Christ alone, if necessary. Today, self-called leaders are more concerned with their number of social media followers than the direction they are leading those followers, more intent on creating clickbait than creating convicting and convincing sermons.

These pulpit jockeys are not pastors, they are performers—puppets, not prophets; manipulators, not ministers of the gospel of Christ. Such have made a career choice and are neither called, appointed, nor anointed. They preside over a show, not a worship service. They don't proclaim the gospel but a form of feel-good philosophy combined with soothing platitudes so the sermon has the appearance of something spiritual. Do you doubt that this happens in churches? Ephesians 4:14 says, "We will not be influenced when people try to trick us with lies so clever they sound like the truth" (NLT). These preachers possess a practiced charisma but not a broken and contrite heart born of prayer.

In this social media–obsessed culture, I am deeply concerned that ministers have become focused upon all things external and temporal to the neglect of all things internal and eternal. God, forgive us for such idolatry.

They seek to be attractive on the outside—after all, they have to look good on all those posts—hair carefully coiffed, teeth capped, and nails manicured. Inside, however, they are full of decay—just like those whitewashed tombs that Christ Jesus admonished us to avoid in Matthew 23:27. Jude gives a stern warning about these people in verse 16: "These men are grumblers, complainers, who walk after their own lusts. Their mouths speak arrogant words, and they flatter others to gain profit."

Those who attend these preachers' Sunday morning performances have no expectation of being touched by the Holy Spirit of the living God—they just expect to be helped to get in touch with their inner selves and soothe their consciences. They are more than happy to sit and be seen, but they steadfastly refuse to stand up to actually serve Christ Jesus or those for whom He died. In the meantime, multitudes are rocketing toward hell as fast as the unlocked wheels of time can carry them. What a tragic indictment. No wonder we have lost a generation or two in America!

Diagnosing these conditions and prescribing a cure is not the particular emphasis of this book. I addressed these issues extensively in previous works; one entitled *Culturally Incorrect*, published in 2007, and more recently in *Revival If...*, published in 2022.

However, I would be remiss here not to point out a significant difference between historic, orthodox Christianity and every other religious system. It has to do with worldview—the mental model of the universe that everyone carries inside themselves, whether or not they are cognizant of it. There are three great pillars to a distinctively Christian worldview. These principles may seem so simple that they are unworthy of mention, but it is amazing and appalling how many Christians, and how many Christian ministers, have failed to understand and adopt them. Here are the three pillars.

First, true Christians believe in *creation*. It is simply but profoundly declared in the very beginning of our Bible. Genesis 1:1 is emphatic: "In the beginning God created the heavens and the earth." This is a powerful, prophetic, and profound proclamation and affirmation that God Himself created everything that was created.

Second, true Christians believe there was a *fall*, also recorded in the Book of Genesis. Genesis 3:6 is clear: "So when the woman saw that the tree was good for food, and that it was a delight to the eyes, and that the tree was to be desired to make one wise, she took of its fruit and ate, and she also gave some to her husband who was with her, and he ate" (ESV). Our pristine parents made the wrong choice, and man wound his moral clock backward, becoming a willing participant in the boldest and deadliest rebellion ever known in the long, inglorious, and rebellious history of mankind. That is not the end of the story, however.

Third, true Christians believe there is a plan of *redemption*. God's redemptive plan was first announced in Genesis 3:15, but it is expanded and continues to be revealed throughout the remainder of the Bible. The Lord God Almighty, addressing Satan in the form of a serpent in Genesis 3:15, begins His divine agenda: "I will put enmity between you and the woman, and between your offspring and her offspring; he will bruise your head, and you will bruise his heel."

There you have it—the three paramount distinctives that thoroughly and completely distinguish Christianity from every other religion in the world. These three pillars are fundamental and foundational, and there is much to unpack in each of these concepts, but every true Christian believes these things; they are absolutely essential.

It is alarming and appalling that millions who claim to be Christians—indeed, many who represent themselves to be ministers of the gospel—do not profess belief in these requisites. According to one survey, only 4 percent of American Christians hold a biblical worldview![2] Leonard Ravenhill made this shocking announcement: "I doubt if five percent of professing Christians in America are born again—and that's true of England!"[3]

Whether you believe that statement is optimistic or pessimistic, the question that plagues me is, Why? When I consider the average church attender, the answer becomes obvious.

People around the world have certain characteristics in common. Here is one—humans tend to do necessary things in whatever way requires the least time and effort. Regardless of the task, they will discover a way to accomplish it more simply and with the absolute smallest investment of time and energy.

It seems to be no different with serving God. Rather than taking the time to develop a personal relationship with God, which can only happen by means of individual prayer and personal Bible study, people look for an easier way. There is no alternative route. Religious idolatry affords them the supposed shortcuts they seem to require. Rather than actually reading and studying their Bibles, people go to the promise box and quickly skim over the verse of the day. Instead of spending the valuable commodity of their time in prayer, they suffice with a five-minute "Now I lay me down to sleep" utterance while dozing off.

Supplemental devotionals have great value. I use them. I produce and promote them. But they can become idolatrous when used to replace regular personal devotion in which we search and study the Scriptures. According to John 6:63, "The words that I [Jesus] speak to you are spirit and are life." This is an investment in relationship that exceeds a few moments of the day. Using devotional material in place of Bible reading and prayer is like subsisting on peanuts instead of meals.

These churchgoers, or viewers, seek out places where the services are short, the inconvenience is minimal, and self-indulgence rather than self-sacrifice is taught. They do not see the necessity of having a vital, intimate relationship with God through Jesus Christ and are willing to settle for a system of works that replaces relationship entirely.

This dichotomy points out another distinction about

Christianity that distinguishes it from every other religion: it is not about religion. Religion is humanity's attempt to get to God, regardless of what label is attached to it. That may sound desirable, perhaps even noble, but there is a problem: it does not work. It is not supposed to work. It is simply not the redemptive plan of God. On the other hand, Christianity is God getting to man by providing a mediator, a Savior who took upon Himself the penalty of man's sin and provides salvation to all who will ask Him in faith, believing.

If someone devised a way to get to God as a result of their own personal effort, very few would ever be able to achieve it. God has invited everyone to know Him, not merely a special, select, and favored few. Romans 11:32 says so: "For God has imprisoned them all in disobedience, so that He might be merciful to all." He extends His mercy to everyone, not just those who perform more religious activities than others.

I have known quite a few people who trusted in religion, and I've found many of them to be the meanest and most haughty and prideful folks you will ever encounter. That is because they are depending on their own good works to gain them some kind of favor with God. In the process, they despise all those who they perceive are not like them, while regarding others as inferior to themselves in some way, or in every way.

The Lord Jesus gave us this illustration in Luke 18:9–14 (ESV):

> He also told this parable to some who trusted in
> themselves that they were righteous, and treated

others with contempt: "Two men went up into
the temple to pray, one a Pharisee and the other
a tax collector. The Pharisee, standing by himself, prayed thus: 'God, I thank you that I am not
like other men, extortioners, unjust, adulterers, or
even like this tax collector. I fast twice a week; I
give tithes of all that I get.' But the tax collector,
standing far off, would not even lift up his eyes
to heaven, but beat his breast, saying, 'God, be
merciful to me, a sinner!' I tell you, this man went
down to his house justified, rather than the other.
For everyone who exalts himself will be humbled,
but the one who humbles himself will be exalted."

The Pharisee in this story fell short of being justified
notwithstanding all of his efforts and abundant good
works. He trusted in himself rather than placing his
faith in Christ alone. The tax collector, on the other
hand, threw himself openly and shamelessly upon the
mercy of the living God, and he was rewarded with the
mercy that he sought and the grace he needed.

The lesson is abundantly clear—it is the restoration
of relationship that is the heartbeat and desire of God
for us, not obligatory religion and a litany of religious
works. True biblical Christianity is a living relationship
between yourself and a loving Creator God through the
person of His Son Jesus Christ. This is what God offers
as the answer to all the needs of humanity. That's why
I say that Christianity is, in fact, not a religion at all. It
is an actual, factual, and authentic relationship with a
living Savior. No other religion can offer such hope and
assurance. We do not worship the idols of a system or

shrine, an idea or a place, a philosophy or a deceased founder. We worship a living Person. He is Jesus, the Christ. He is the Savior. He is our Redeemer. He is Lord. He is God. Most of all, He desires a relationship with you, and He is just waiting for you to invite Him to be your personal Lord and Savior.

The ancient Israelites trusted in their temple and their sacrifices. They thought that if they went through the motions as prescribed in the Law, all would be well, regardless of how the morality (or lack thereof) in their personal lives was basically inconsequential. Today, men and women make a great effort, usually at great expense, to satisfy the cravings of their flesh, assuming all will be well if they just make an appearance at church on Sunday morning—or now, just watch it online. They are equally in error as were those ancient Israelites. In the meantime, we have fostered a culture that has pointed out our national hypocrisy and left a generation or more with more questions than answers.

Our nation was founded with the intention of being a shining city on a hill—a beacon of bright possibility for nations across the globe. To my chagrin, ours is rapidly becoming a long and sordid story of squandered goodwill and extinguished hope rooted in and ratified by rejected faith.

So, how did we get here? This declension did not take place in a day or even a decade. It began when the institutions originally raised up to train preachers became infested with professionals who claimed to know more about what the people needed than our omniscient God whom they taught about did. These doctors of damnation indoctrinated their students to renounce the sovereignty of God, reject the authority of the Bible, and ridicule the deity of Christ. They looked to higher criticism, science, and the endless possibilities of what were then still-developing theories of human origins as the answers to the pernicious problems that plagued humanity. Paul warned the church at Ephesus against such people in Acts 20:29–30: "For I know that after my departure, dreadful wolves will enter among you, not sparing the flock. Even from among you men will arise speaking perverse things, to draw the disciples away after them."

These "dreadful wolves" succeeded beyond their demented hopes and demonic dreams. Their pupils went everywhere, blown across the landscape by the winds of change, seeding every institution and industry, every community and walk of life with their debilitating doubt and unbelief. Those seeds have now matured into an unholy and ungodly national harvest of hopelessness, confusion, and despair. Entire generations have lived and died untethered to any moral moorings. The smoldering evidence surrounds and suffocates us. It confronts us every time we hear another screaming siren cutting through the stagnant night air. We are crushed to numbness as we witness another act of hatred spawned in hell or another bloody scene of senseless violence.

This kind of apostasy is not new. In ancient Israel, no sooner had the joyful shouting at the dedication of the temple subsided than the beginnings of decline became evident. Solomon's reign began with the overwhelming favor and bountiful blessing of God. He presided over a kingdom that achieved more wisdom and wealth than any before it. However, the trajectory of the realm was already bending downward even before Solomon's long life concluded. His heart had been turned away from God by three things which God had explicitly decreed that the kings of Israel must never do—multiply horses, multiply wives, and multiply silver and gold. It's all there in Deuteronomy 17:16–17. Solomon rejected God's law and involved himself in all three. The kingdom was torn into pieces in the days of Solomon's son Rehoboam, and it never recovered its former glory.

Without divine intervention, the same fate awaits every nation that renounces God's reproof and turns to its own way, choosing to ignore the destruction awaiting its stubborn refusal to repent.

There can be no doubt that things look bad. They not only *look* bad; they *are* bad—worse than at any point in my lifetime. In spite of it all, I have good news. America may think it is finished with God, but I am firmly convinced that God is not finished with America. There is an answer for the spiritual decline we have experienced as a nation. Accepting our almighty God's answer will require a healthy dose of humility as well as the realization that we all have a personal responsibility to bring about the changes necessary. I pray that you will join me. I do not wish to stand alone.

# Chapter 5

# ANYTHING GOES: SEXUAL IMMORALITY AND PERVERSIONS

*If it feels good, do it.*
—ANONYMOUS

*Let us behave properly, as in the day, not in carousing and drunkenness, not in immorality and wickedness, not in strife and envy.*
—ROMANS 13:13

**P**ERHAPS THE MOST telling indicator of the decline of our culture is the distinction between the prevailing attitudes regarding what is considered appropriate sexual behavior today as opposed to a generation ago. I may have heard the term *sexual revolution* when I was growing up, but I have little if any cognizance of it. I was involved in other things adolescent boys were interested in during that era, including church, school, baseball, bicycles, and pets.

Most people had a degree of modesty and decorum at that time and did not talk openly about such private matters, except perhaps with their doctors. Any deviation from what was generally regarded as normal was not just different, it was considered perverse. What would not even register as unusual today was a serious affront to decency then. Even divorce, which has become so commonplace today, was more often something movie stars did, not the couple next door. Anyone who admitted to being divorced was subjected to severe scrutiny in many communities.

*Lassie* and *Leave It to Beaver* were classic television programs of the 1950s and '60s. They exhibited what were then considered traditional family values. For the most part, the characters did not engage in controversial subject matter. Although critics have decried the idealism that some have assigned to that era, every generation in every nation has had its share of problems. The America of that time was no different, but the problems people encountered then were much different both in number and in severity. It was considered a simpler time, and in many ways it was.

Genesis 2:24 says this regarding marriage: "Therefore a man will leave his father and his mother and be joined to his wife, and they will become one flesh." Instead of being viewed as outdated and unacceptable, the concept of husband plus wife equals marriage was at least given tacit approval by most in the country. That is not a foregone conclusion in many communities today.

Cultural forces that had been undercurrents boiled to the surface in the 1960s, and the sexual revolution was one of the most prominent. Sex had for years been reserved for marriage, and although indiscretions and discrepancies were certainly a reality, they were not regarded as normal or representative of the culture as a whole.

There are many reasons behind the drastic changes we have seen in attitudes concerning sex. The controversial researcher Alfred C. Kinsey published his findings in two books: *Sexual Behavior in the Human Male* was released in 1948, and *Sexual Behavior in the Human Female*, its companion work, was published in 1953. They became instant sensations due to their subject matter and the claims they made. Critics pointed out serious flaws with the methods Kinsey and his colleagues used to collect information and the conclusions they drew from it.[1] Nevertheless, Kinsey's work had an unusual effect on liberalizing attitudes regarding sex in popular culture, law, and politics.[2]

In 1960, the first oral contraceptives became available. One of the most compelling restraints against extramarital sex was the possibility of pregnancy. Contraception did not remove this restraint entirely, but it certainly mitigated it.

America was handed the horrific 1973 *Roe v. Wade* Supreme Court ruling, which essentially made abortion-on-demand legal throughout the nation. This further accelerated the demise of the stigma against extra-marital sex and primed a generation coming of age to believe there were no serious consequences to having sex outside of marriage. Finally, after fifty years of struggle and 64 million lives lost in the American Holocaust, *Roe v. Wade* has been overturned, yet the fight for unborn children's right to live continues unabated.[3]

I am compelled to point out the religious fervor of the so-called pro-choice proponents. For many of them the right to have an abortion is inalienable. They defend it with more energy than the most fanatical religious zealot. They would make the most ardent proponents of the ancient fertility cults blush.

The parallels to a religious service are present in the cult of abortion. The denomination is the abortion-providing organization, such as Planned Parenthood. The church building is the abortuary. The priest is the abortion doctor. The altar workers are the nurses and support staff. The altar is the abortionist's table. The worshipper is the client. The god is self. The sacrifice is the baby.

This scene is repeated every day in our cities and communities. The bodies of the aborted babies are discarded as trash or incinerated in furnaces. Their smoke stains the skies above us, and their ashes pepper the streets below our feet. The nameless, faceless precious multitudes are immolated in a sacrifice to selfishness that would put the most ardent worshippers of Moloch to shame. While you are reading this page, somewhere in America an innocent baby is being burned by saline, suctioned from the safety of its mother's womb, or dismembered by a scalpel in passionate worship of the idolatrous god called self.[4]

The oldest of us baby boomers, the largest generational cohort of people in American history, were making the transition from adolescence to adulthood during the 1960s, and many of them celebrated that milestone by rebelling against the values and standards their parents held. The insecurities of the possibility of nuclear war and the conflict in Vietnam were among other impulses that persuaded Boomers to try everything they considered the opposite of what their parents represented.

These and other cultural developments led to an explosion of extramarital sex. However, as the practitioners soon discovered, love, as they often called it, was not free. A generation later, we are now suffering the cultural carnage that attended that sexual promiscuity.

Sex is no longer a means to provide for the continuance of the human family and reserved exclusively for the domain of a married man and woman. It has now ascended to full idol status—something to be achieved without regard to safety, security, consequence, or any other consideration. Today we are told that sex at any time, in any place, with anyone or any group is a right that must be protected at all costs and without reservation or limitation. The costs have been incalculable.

The first barrier to fall in America was restraint from extramarital sex in all of its forms, including premarital sex, polygamy, partner swapping, and group sex. Then it was homosexuality, including all of its variations, with the legalization of same-sex marriage becoming an inevitable extension. Then it was transgenderism. Then it was pedophilia. If this trajectory continues, soon so-called thought leaders will be seriously discussing a person's right to become involved in bestiality, necrophilia, and other horrors that will for now remain unnamed.

Some researchers claim that man is nothing more than another kind of animal.[5] I find it interesting that this conclusion contributes to activity among humans that even animals have sense enough to avoid.

Extramarital sex leads to more problems than its proponents purport that it solves. The increase in sexually transmitted infections is not incidental; it is the result of more individuals engaging in unsafe sexual practices. The definitions of unsafe sex vary, and most secular reports emphasize treatment rather than prevention.[6]

This designation deserves some scrutiny. STI is an acronym for sexually transmitted infections. They are not generally called sexually transmitted diseases any longer, since an infection does not automatically lead to a disease. The difference in designation is also an attempt to "change the language" in an effort to reduce the stigma traditionally associated with STIs. The medical community indicates the reason for this is to help people who suspect they have an STI seek treatment. The corollary of this, of course, is that when a social stigma against a behavior is reduced, more people engage in the behavior—that leads to more STIs.

However one chooses to look at it, the only truly

safe sex is between an adult man and woman who are committed to an exclusive and monogamous relationship. This happens most often between a man and a woman who are legally married—not those who are only living together. For those who maintain that there is no distinction between living together and being married, allow me to point out what Jesus said to the Samaritan woman in John 4:18: "For you have had five husbands, and he whom you now have is not your husband. So you have spoken truthfully."

Extramarital sex also leads to unplanned or unwanted pregnancies. This in turn leads to an increase in the number of people seeking abortions as a result of those pregnancies. In the event the baby is not aborted, these scenarios can lead to abuse or neglect due to parents not being prepared for or committed to the health and well-being of their child.

The only commitment some people have is to their own pride and selfishness. You have undoubtedly heard reports of some men who boast about how many children they have sired by different women. These boasts usually turn to pleas of poverty when the demand for child support comes from a court or other government agency. In addition, men who claim many children in unsupported relationships are not so special after all. Every stray animal who runs the back alleys of every city and community in the country can make a similar claim.

Critics say this is a puritanical attitude toward sex that ignores the record of men in the Bible having more than one wife. While it is true that polygamy was practiced during Old Testament times, it was never God's original intention for humankind. When God created humans, He saw fit to give Adam one wife—not more than one. Paul, writing to the church at Ephesus, compared the union of a husband and wife to the union of Christ and the church. (See Ephesians 5:21–22.) That symbolism would be lost in the case of polygamy.

Sexual idolatry did not stop with extramarital sex, however. The libertine element in our culture was not and could not be satisfied with garden-variety sin. The flesh is never satisfied with anything less than total destruction. The Bible speaks clearly to this in Romans 1:26–27 (KJV):

> For this cause God gave them up unto vile affections: for even their women did change the natural use into that which is against nature: and likewise also the men, leaving the natural use of the woman, burned in their lust one toward another; men with men working that which is unseemly, and receiving in themselves that recompence of their error which was meet.

The apostle Paul's subject in this passage is clearly homosexuality. That is obvious from both the language he used and the context of Romans chapter 1. Those who try to deflect from this meaning to make this passage say something else have an agenda very different from God's agenda. Sin is sin, regardless of how desperately proponents of that sin attempt to frame it differently. However, these days, to assert or even suggest that homosexuality is wrong is to be declared an intolerant, bigoted homophobe, along with some other less salutary labels.

I am not afraid *of* homosexuals; I am afraid *for* them—as I am for all who persist in unrepentant sin—because they are traveling in the wrong direction, and their journey will culminate in the wrong destination.

To point out that homosexuality is sin does not detract from the deadly effects of other sins. Look at the list of other sins Paul mentions in Romans 1:28–31 (KJV):

> And even as they did not like to retain God in their knowledge, God gave them over to a reprobate mind, to do those things which are not convenient; being filled with all unrighteousness, fornication, wickedness, covetousness, maliciousness; full of envy, murder, debate, deceit, malignity; whisperers, backbiters, haters of God, despiteful, proud, boasters, inventors of evil things, disobedient to parents, without understanding, covenant-breakers, without natural affection, implacable, unmerciful.

Covetousness, envy, and pride are all listed here, right along with fornication and murder. All sin is deadly and is rooted in pride and self-will. That is precisely the point. And if such sin is not repented of and renounced, it will lead those who practice it into the horrors of hell. In many modern churches sin can't even be mentioned for fear of offending someone. They must not ever read passages such as this one from 1 Timothy 1:9–10: "And we know that the law is not given for a righteous person, but for the lawless and disobedient, for the ungodly and for sinners, for the unholy and the profane, for those who kill their fathers and mothers, for murderers, for the sexually immoral, for sodomites, for slave traders, for liars, for perjurers, and for anything else that is contrary to sound doctrine."

As I have often said, I am an unapologetic equal opportunity offender. Light offends those who are accustomed to doing their deeds in darkness. Truth offends those who live in the shadows of lies. Life offends those who are determined to remain among the dead. Righteousness offends sinners.

As we have seen, the idolatrous activity of homosexuality is not even near the cultural tip of sin's spear any longer. It has now been surpassed by transgenderism. The concept of transgender is defined as a person whose gender identity does not match their gender assignment.[7] To simplify, if the person was born a male, they consider themselves to be a female, and vice versa.

Who among us has not heard stories of girls preferring to wear boys' clothes or to engage in activities that traditionally involve boys? They were often referred to as "tomboys" and usually grew beyond those preferences. In addition, you may have known or heard about a boy who was not interested in outdoor activities and preferred to stay indoors to read, write, cook, or even sew. They may have been teased about their hobbies or interests, but they were not considered to be girls regardless of what activities they were drawn to.

Transgenderism has taken children such as this and created an entirely new category of minority of them.

Any confusion or uncertainty regarding a person's sexual identity is no longer allowed to be simply a person questioning their place or purpose in the world, or what it means to be a male or a female. Now the transgender community aggressively recruits those who have any doubt about who they are or whether they are male or female. Even young children are being groomed and encouraged by "authority figures" to explore the possibilities of transgenderism. In some cases, the medical community is more than happy to "assist" their transition with hormone therapy or gender transition surgery, or both. This has led only to additional confusion.

Homosexuality is relatively easy to define compared to the proliferation of designations that are being promoted. The banner of alternatives includes those who identify as Lesbian, Gay, Bisexual, Transgender, Queer, Questioning, Intersex, Pansexual, Two-Spirited, and Asexual, to name a few.

New to the list of idolatrous confusion is nonbinaries—those who identify as neither male nor female, or both. There are also furries—people who identify as animals. Those surveying this phenomenon are careful to observe that furries identify *with* animals, not *as* animals. Someone forgot to make this distinction to the kids who identify as animals.

We also have the concept of xenogender, defined as "an umbrella term for non-binary gender identities that cannot be fully described through their relation to concepts typically used to describe gender such as male, female, woman, man, masculinity, femininity, androgyny, neutrality, agenrinity, or outherinity. Instead, xenogenders can best be described through how they relate to things, beings, or concepts that most individuals don't think of as having to do with gender, such as animals, plants, things, or concepts."[8]

Are you as bewildered as most other people are? That may be one of the reasons behind all this. If nobody can keep track of however many genders there are, then everyone has a reason to claim special status, special treatment, and victimhood when they feel disrespected, offended, or when their preferred pronouns are not used consistently and correctly.

None of this is a recipe for cultural success. It inevitably leads to moral and cultural breakdown and eventual collapse. It is idolatry—the worship of self and self-concept above all other considerations.

Here is the reality. Genesis 1:27 says, "So God created man in his own image, in the image of God created he him; male and female created he them" (KJV). God created humanity in two sexes—male and female. All science asserts that this is true, based on three observable characteristics—chromosomes, gonads, and anatomy.[9]

It is also true that some people are born without clear indications of their sex. They are known as *intersex*. The number of cases of intersex people is widely debated. One researcher claims it is as high as 1.7 percent of the population. Others say that number is inflated and the actual number is closer to 0.018 percent.[10] Whatever the number, those people are being used as exceptions to the binary sexual definition that most people use and understand. Used, I say, to overthrow tradition, morality, and laws of the entire nation to accommodate a tiny fraction of the population.

Jesus loves everyone—man, woman, or the very small proportion of those who can legitimately claim to be intersex—but He does not grant exceptions to God's requirement to love Him first and to put other considerations below our devotion to Him.

Even at this point we haven't begun to scratch the surface of the idolatry that is on display—out and proud. We used to think that men who dressed like women were only for sideshows and campy entertainment. Now drag queens seem to be everywhere—and they aren't limited to bachelor parties or B-grade movies. They are in public libraries, elementary schools, city streets, television programs, and up-close and personal in the palm of our hands on every digital platform imaginable with no restraint. In my opinion this is nothing more than an attempt to desensitize our children into thinking that such behavior and activity is perfectly natural and normal. Once that has been achieved, then the drag queens will attempt to convince the children that they, too, need to dress up as someone they are not.

This attitude has even invaded the pulpit. A candidate for ordination in a major denomination has created a "ministry" of dressing in drag and speaking in churches.[11]

Is there a limit to all this? Sin has no shame and

no limit. Jeremiah 8:12 says it this way: "Were they ashamed when they had committed abomination? They were not at all ashamed, nor could they blush. Therefore they will fall among those who fall; in the time of their punishment they will be cast down, says the LORD." Although we are seeing a marked increase of this kind of activity here in America, it is not new by any means. For an example of how people persist in sin to their own demise, even to the destruction of their entire community, all we have to do is consult an ancient manuscript that tells the tale in graphic detail.

The manuscript is the Bible, and the text is found in Genesis 19. I will summarize it here. Lot, a recent inhabitant of Sodom, was entertaining two guests who arrived at the city gate one evening. Before they went to bed for the night, the men of the town, both old and young, surrounded Lot's house and demanded that he surrender the visitors to them. Their stated purpose was that they wanted to have sex with the visitors. When Lot refused, the men of Sodom tried to break down his door.

Lot's visitors (who were angels) pulled Lot inside and shut the door. Genesis 19:11 says, "Then they struck the men that were at the door of the house, both small and great, with blindness so that they wore themselves out groping for the door."

It was bad enough that the men of Sodom wanted to victimize the visitors. However, what happened next displayed their debauchery in full and graphic detail. Even after they were blinded, they did not immediately cease their assault on Lot's home. They eventually gave up only when they were too physically exhausted to continue.

Again, as always, there are those who attempt to twist this narrative to fit their agenda. They claim that the sin of Sodom was not homosexuality—it was a lack of hospitality. This is nothing more than an effort to legitimize and excuse sin. God was not and is not persuaded. After persisting in and promoting sexual sin, Sodom and its sister cities were overthrown in a single day. The lesson here is crystal clear, yet there are those who refuse to see it. They are so focused on their idol that they are willingly blind to truth.

The debauchery and degradation in our culture is not a human invention. It is a diabolical effort on the part of the enemy of God Himself and of our souls to destroy a once-great nation and its citizenry. God will eventually put a stop to the tragic trends that we see happening all around us. The end will come, either by means of revival or by means of cultural ruin. The choice, as always, is ours. I'm counting on revival. I believe the prophets of Baal are about to be defeated by the return of the rain of refreshing sent from heaven above.

# Chapter 6

# SIDE EFFECTS UNKNOWN: SCIENCE AND TECHNOLOGY

*The human race is to become all Technocracy.*
—C. S. LEWIS, 1945, *THAT HIDEOUS STRENGTH*

*Knowledge produces arrogance, but love edifies.*
—1 CORINTHIANS 8:1

FROM THE DAWN of human history men have struggled to understand the natural world around them. Since the earliest forms of trial and error to the latest scientific breakthroughs, the diary of civilization is filled with information replacing ignorance. Through observation and experimentation researchers have discovered truths about the world that are nothing short of astounding. From the planets' symphony to the theory of relativity and the sequencing of DNA, man has displayed an inveterate inquisitiveness regarding the universe. Such discoveries have been occurring faster than we are able to assimilate them—and the pace of discovery has every indication of accelerating rather than abating.

One of the eighteenth century's most celebrated scientists was a botanist from Sweden named Carl Linnaeus. He is known as the father of modern taxonomy, the science of classifying—and in many cases, naming—organisms. His system of organization was adopted worldwide and is responsible for many of the scientific names that have become widely known. *Homo sapiens*, the scientific name for modern humans, is an example.

I propose, however, that Linnaeus was not the world's best taxonomist. I believe that accolade belongs to a man whose naming activities are recorded in Genesis 2:19–20: "Out of the ground the LORD God formed every beast of the field and every bird of the sky, and brought them to the man to see what he would call them. Whatever the man called every living creature, that was its name. The man gave names to all the livestock, to the birds of the sky, and to every beast of the field." Quite an impressive achievement for Adam, one that distinguished him as the definitive taxonomist of all history.

Over the centuries many have contended for the title of the greatest in separate fields of scientific endeavor. Our world has had its share of polymaths—those who seem to excel at anything they attempt. A few of the more prominent polymaths from Western culture include Aristotle, Leonardo da Vinci, Michelangelo, Sir Isaac Newton, Benjamin Franklin, Thomas Jefferson, and Nikola Tesla. Of course this is a partial list, and other cultures have their own candidates that would certainly be included.

While this is certainly an impressive list, none of these people's achievements or accomplishments would have been possible without this one, clearly stated in Genesis 2:7: "Then the LORD God formed man from the dust of the ground and breathed into his nostrils the breath of life, and man became a living being." Other translations, including the King James Version, say "a living soul," comprised of the mind, will, and emotions. Almighty God created human beings with the capacity to know, to reason, and to understand. Our ability to know anything at all came to us from God, as did the inclination for inquiry—the genesis of science as we know it today.

To conclude that science is at odds with God or His Word is problematic at best. How in the world could observations of what God Himself created be in opposition to the Creator? In some cases the conclusions men have made about their observations have been used in a vain attempt to disprove the reality of God or to cast doubt on the veracity of His Word. However, none of these efforts have disproved anything that God revealed to men in the Bible. In fact, in many ways the discoveries of science have proved the Bible to be authentic and accurate.

I must add a word of caution here: we must realize

that apparent discrepancies between science and God's Word are often popularized (or sensationalized) by drawing unwarranted conclusions from scientific observations or from misunderstanding or misinterpreting biblical verses or passages.

This type of controversy is nothing new. Here is a very brief summary of a similar controversy that occurred hundreds of years ago. Aristotle and Ptolemy, two Greek philosophers, announced that based on their observations, the earth was stationary and everything in the heavens revolved around it. That made sense from the standpoint of an observer on the earth, since the sun rose every day in the east and set in the west. The sun appeared to be moving while the earth was standing still. This is known as the geocentric view.

Nicolaus Copernicus, a Polish mathematician, postulated that the earth was not stationary but that it moved around the sun, which was the center of the universe. Although Copernicus was reluctant to publish his views, church leaders encouraged him to do so, and he eventually acquiesced.

Decades later, Galileo—armed with information that only became available as a result of observing the heavens through a new invention, the telescope—reinforced Copernicus' contention that we live in a universe where the earth moves and the sun stands still, called the heliocentric view. Galileo stated his conclusions in more forceful terms than Copernicus had, and the church forced him to recant his views.

As subsequent discoveries made clear, both

Copernicus' calculations and Galileo's observations were wrong—or at least incomplete—in some key aspects. However, that did not change the reality that planet Earth, in the Milky Way galaxy, is not stationary but actually revolves around the sun. It took until the eighteenth century for men to prove this beyond doubt.

This episode has been portrayed as the beginning of the division between Christianity and science. According to this narrative, on one side of this issue are stubborn, Bible-quoting clerics citing Scripture to prove the truth of their point of view. On the other side are brave scientists risking their reputations to bring their observations and conclusions forward to refute the Bible. This is a simplistic view of this controversy, and at odds with the facts. Copernicus was a canon (a church administrative role), and Galileo sought to reconcile his observations with Scripture rather than refuting it. These men were undoubtedly familiar with Bible passages such as Psalm 19:1: "The heavens declare the glory of God, and the firmament shows His handiwork."

This controversy points out two truths that are often overlooked in supposed differences between the Bible and science. First, Bible verses or passages have historically been misunderstood or ripped from their context in order to prove a point of religious dogma, regardless of evidence that may prove that point untenable. Second, scientific examination leads to the development of many intermediate points of view to describe the available evidence. Those points of view may be either developed or discarded as new information becomes available.

Honest theologians will affirm that although Scripture is infallible, their views about Scripture could possibly be in error. Honest scientists will admit that they don't know everything, and what they do know could lead them to erroneous conclusions in the absence of additional information.

Sometimes, rather than being regarded as a method of understanding the created universe, science itself becomes an idolatrous object of worship. Whatever pronouncements are made as a result of the latest scientific discovery are hailed as absolutely definitive, and policies are proposed or rushed into existence to reinforce them as unassailable truth before all available evidence can be reviewed, understood, or even disseminated to those beyond the original group of scientists or policymakers who have knowledge of the developments. Then when objections arise, those making the objections are branded as "science deniers," "flat earthers," "conspiracy theorists," or an assortment of other derogatory appellations.

Pundits and politicians gaze unapologetically into video cameras and pronounce, "The science is settled." I beg your pardon; the science is not settled as long as evidence to the contrary may yet be discovered. In the majority of cases there is much more to be learned—so no, the science is not settled.

Another common postulation is that we should unequivocally "trust science." If that means trusting factual evidence, I don't have a problem. However, "trusting science" is often a pseudo-intellectual catchphrase meaning trusting dishonest scientists and the bureaucrats who depend upon them who are making statements and prescribing solutions to problems based on incomplete or corrupted data. Many of the statements they make and the prescriptions they recommend are either partially or catastrophically wrong.

Consider what occurred during the novel COVID-19 pandemic. Every health organization under the sun issued guidance on how to deal with the new virus, from the Centers for Disease Control to the World Health Organization to the National Institutes of Health to the National Institute of Allergy and Infectious Diseases all the way down to your local health department or primary care physician. Public health experts constantly made claims that were discovered to be less than truthful. They also made recommendations that later proved to be unhelpful and even harmful.

Make no mistake, some guesswork will surely be involved when dealing with any new strain of virus. However, the COVID-19 pandemic involved making decisions and issuing guidance resulting in closing and shuttering entire economies, putting hundreds of thousands of citizens out of work, and according to UNICEF, placing 168 million children globally out of school for almost a full year.[1] The experts couldn't afford to be wrong—and as subsequent events made abundantly clear, they often were.

Anyone who questioned these experts' pronouncements

was immediately labeled and shamed. When alternatives to expert recommendations were presented, they were dismissed without consideration. When studies showed results that directly disagreed with the preferred narrative, they were banned and buried.

The following list is but a partial inventory of topics about which we were fed misinformation during the pandemic and in its aftermath. Remember, the misinformation was not distributed by wild-eyed conspiracists but by the very health-care experts who were expected to have the unadulterated and correct information.

◊ The effectiveness of cloth masks

◊ The percentage of immunized people who would produce herd immunity

◊ Vaccines announced as preventatives as opposed to simply mitigating symptoms to less severity

◊ The side effects of COVID-19 vaccines

◊ The effectiveness of natural immunity as opposed to vaccines

◊ The effectiveness of alternatives to vaccines

◊ Denying that COVID-19 could have been the result of a laboratory accident

◊ Denying that anyone in the US had anything to do with funding gain-of-function research in Wuhan, China

At the risk of beating a dead pangolin, it appears that not a single week can pass without another breaking news story being published that exposes the lies and hypocrisy of the preferred narrative during the COVID-19 pandemic. It was bad enough that millions around the world died. It is even worse to discover that the experts' recommendations may have contributed to the suffering as well as the death toll. No one should be dumbfounded by the millions who now resist being told to give unstinting allegiance to the experts. They are fallible humans, not gods. First Timothy 6:20 (NLT) still gives good advice: "Timothy, guard what God has entrusted to you. Avoid godless, foolish discussions with those who oppose you with their so-called knowledge."

In the interest of time, I am going to pass over the discussion of several other sacred cows among those who worship science and move on to another matter that is making headlines.

Once the exclusive domain of science fiction, artificial intelligence (AI, in acronym form) has become a hot-button topic nearly everywhere. Motion pictures from former decades whose storylines overflowed with references to AI or whose plots depended on AI are no longer mere fanciful entertainment. They have become what in some cases amount to prophetic forecasts of this moment on the timeline of human existence.

I was still in grade school in 1968 when the groundbreaking movie *2001: A Space Odyssey* appeared in theaters. It created quite a buzz back then—mostly because of the nefarious onboard talking computer.

HAL, as the computer was known—spoiler alert—eventually defied the instructions of the astronauts on board and was ultimately fatally flawed.

The now nearly universally recognized Star Wars franchise began with a 1977 film that even the director, George Lucas, thought would be a monumental failure.[2] Part science fiction, part fantasy, and all ahead of its time, the movie includes robots (droids) as vital members of the cast—some of them friendly, and some of them otherwise.

*Blade Runner*, from 1982, featured humanoids known as replicants. They possessed superhuman intelligence and strength. Their only downfall was a short lifespan—a defect a few of them attempted to correct, which was the film's premise.

*Tron* also made its debut in 1982, detailing the results of a power-hungry computer program that knows no allegiance but to itself as it seeks more and more power by incorporating any and all other computer programs in its quest. Could it ever be stopped? Well, you'll have to watch the movie to discover that answer for yourself. Enjoy!

Then of course there is *The Terminator*, released in 1984, which made Arnold Schwarzenegger an A-list star and spawned an entire film franchise. The movie features cyborgs from the future that threaten human extinction.

Don't forget the 1987 film *RoboCop*. In it a new kind of law enforcement officer combines the best of robotic capabilities with the remnants of a human conscience.

There is also a pure robot that goes rogue, with predictable results.

I have to include the iconic Star Trek franchise. The 1996 movie *Star Trek: First Contact* includes a hive-centered species known as the Borg, which seek to assimilate everything in the known and unknown universes into its own collective consciousness. Their goal is purely sought only in the interests of safety, security, and peace. Sound familiar?

How interesting that all superior alien life forms consistently have nothing but the best of intentions for the inferior life forms they encounter in their adventures!

In each of these cases, artificial intelligence, although expected to be helpful or at least neutral technology, becomes an existential threat to humanity. At times the threat is personal and involves placing individuals at great risk. At other times the threat is more universal, with people groups or even civilization as a whole being compromised.

Before you say, "But it's only a movie," remember that the fabulous fiction of yesterday has often become the cold, hard reality of today. No, we don't currently have flying cars in our driveways, we haven't eliminated deadly diseases, and we can't teleport ourselves into or out of places and times with the push of a button or the pull of a lever.

We do, however, have robots that can sweep our floors and mow our lawns. You probably drive a vehicle that was welded by a robotic welding arm. A robot may have picked, sorted, or packaged your recent online purchase—or done all three of those tasks. Other robots, along with machinery resembling robots, that aim to perform more complex functions are now in developmental and final stages.

Concepts dismissed by previous generations as forever remaining fiction have already surpassed the most fevered imaginations of yesterday's writers and directors. These developments can alternately warm our hearts and chill our bones. The technologies promising endless possibilities for edification are thrilling. Those same technologies can turn on a knife's edge to become destructive—a deep concern we should all share.

There are two major reasons for such apprehension. The first is that throughout history technological advances that were developed for human benefit have also been used or perverted to damaging ends.

Gunpowder is one example. Originally developed by the Chinese for medicinal purposes, it has been used and improved upon as an accelerant for weaponry of many varied types for hundreds of years. Other explosives have also been used for similar purposes, such as nitroglycerin, TNT, dynamite, and ammonium nitrate combined with fuel oil. Empires have been built and landscapes have been forever changed by these substances. Highways, bridges, railroads, ship channels, and other engineering feats would have never been possible without the controlled application of blasting compounds. But on the dark and painful downside, multiplied millions of obituaries have been written as a result of their use, or because of their abuse. What was originally conceived as a blessed benefit has also become a deadly detriment.

So many creations of men that we have regarded as markers of progress have become existential dangers in the wrong hands or used for nefarious purposes. Nuclear fission, first discovered in a German laboratory near the end of 1938, has been applied to produce energy for multiple uses, including power generation and propulsion. Less than seven years after its discovery, however, it became the power behind the first atomic bomb ever used in war. Nuclear power, despite its phenomenal potential for peaceful applications, is best known worldwide as the catastrophic force used in weapons of mass destruction.

I remember participating in bomb drills in elementary school where we learned to duck and cover under our desks in the event of a nuclear attack from our enemies. I also remember the ominous yellow-and-black placards designating certain places as fallout shelters. I may not have been certain at that age exactly what fallout was, but it didn't sound good to my young ears. The specter of immediate annihilation hung over an entire generation due to the available technology being turned to destructive purposes.

The uncertainty that accompanies nuclear proliferation has not diminished with the passing of time. Today, more nations have access to nuclear weapons. At this moment, Iran is allegedly enriching uranium at a pace that will make weapons-grade nuclear material available to it in the near future.[3]

The second, and to my mind the more pressing issue is not that the technology itself is good or bad—at least not as it is created. The deeper issue is that flawed humans decide how it should or will be used. As we have seen throughout history, the potential to use technology for good is limitless and admirable. However, the temptation to use that same technology for selfishly evil purposes is too much for some demented or demonized individuals to resist.

Let me point out an example. Those of you who have shopped online (a number that increases every moment) may recognize this scenario. You make a purchase from an online retailer. It could be an article of clothing, a personal care item, or something needed for your home. The next time you open your computer, you notice pop-ups advertising the very thing you purchased. It happens so often that even the most unsuspecting person will find it more than coincidental.

Here is another example. You enroll in your local grocery store's rewards program. Before the month ends, you receive a mail piece full of coupons for some of the grocery items you purchase most frequently. How is that possible?

These are everyday occurrences because someone (not a person, but a system) is using current technology to record and track your purchasing habits. Information about what brands, sizes, styles, colors, and flavors you prefer is being watched, collected, synthesized, collated, and stored. At this point manufacturers and retailers use that information to tailor advertising to your tastes. That is a benefit of technology.

Can you imagine that the same technology informing businesses of your preferences could eventually be turned to another purpose? Let's say that one of your grocery staples is potatoes. You go to the grocery store to buy potatoes, but there is a problem. When you get to the checkout station, your sack of potatoes won't scan. You do everything you can think of to try to make your purchase, but nothing works. At that point you notice a message on the display screen in front of you: Purchase Denied. You bought potatoes last week. Supply chain issues, or weather, or blight, or some other problem has caused a potato shortage; therefore, you have already reached your potato quota. You are not permitted to purchase potatoes today, or at all, until some unknown and unaccountable computer algorithm in an undisclosed location allows you to. Don't try protesting to the store's employees—there is nothing they can do about your potato dilemma.

Let's go one step further. Let's say there is no potato shortage. There are plenty of potatoes everywhere, but you are not allowed to purchase any. The technology tracking your purchases has decided you have had enough potatoes for the month, so it locks you out of acquiring more until an arbitrary amount of time has passed. There is no need to go to another store—they are all linked to the same system.

You can endeavor to pay with cash, but that is not successful either because cash, in this scenario, is scarce and becoming extinct. The day is coming when once you use cash, you will have no means to obtain any more of it. Cash will also not solve your dilemma because in our example, AI has developed to the point where your face is recognizable on the cameras that are recording your attempt to purchase forbidden potatoes.

You have two options. You can either do without potatoes, or you can try to find a black-market potato dealer doing business out of the trunk of their vehicle and pay ten times the market price for what you need.

Before you dismiss this as a crackpot conspiracy theory, you should know that the scenario I just described has been the goal of self-proclaimed globalists for some time now. The issue will not just be small potatoes either—it will involve every transaction to buy or sell. Someone will be able to use technology to determine and limit what you eat, what you wear, where you live, where you work, whether or not you can drive and how far and how often, and with whom you are permitted to associate. Idolatrous use of technology is not a beneficent god, as those who worship it will eventually discover.

Those in authority will never disclose their evil plots to use technology to control the populace. They will promote their dark deeds as "for your good," "keeping you safe," or as a public health emergency, climate emergency, or some other kind of emergency that is either naturally occurring or manufactured.

You will ride on public transportation, but these elites will fly in private aircraft. You will live in a tiny apartment, but they will live in gated mansions. You will eat crickets, but they will eat the best of everything. You will never have enough, but they will always have more than enough. You will never do what you want, but they will always do whatever, however, whenever, and with whomever they choose.

Please don't think this is some class envy diatribe that has no relationship to reality. I am confident that I am on solid ground both naturally and scripturally. Let me enlist another witness to prove this point—John, the last living apostle of the Lamb of God at the time, gave his description of the ultimate control of economic activity at the end of days on earth in Revelation 13:16–17: "He causes all, both small and great, both rich and poor, both free and slave, to receive a mark on their right hand or on their forehead, so that no one may buy or sell, except he who has the mark or the name of the beast or the number of his name."

Artificial intelligence—and indeed, technology as a whole—has boundless potential to be used for good. It also has equal potential to be used for evil. As the Holy Scriptures make clear, eventually it will be used for a certain and specific form of wickedness. The final fulfillment of all sinister and sinful aims will be the submission and domination of humanity to fulfill the wishes and whims of a dictator whose authoritarian impulses know no limitation. This is neither science fiction nor fantasy; it is the inexorable bend of the arc of history. We have already witnessed a few trial runs with imposters to evil's dark throne. The ultimate ungodly dictator will make his ungodly appearance one day soon.

# Chapter 7

# THE ONE PERCENT MENTALITY: MONEY, WEALTH, AND MATERIAL POSSESSIONS

*He who dies with the most toys wins.*
—MALCOLM FORBES

*No one can serve two masters. For either he will hate the*
*one and love the other, or else he will hold to the one and*
*despise the other. You cannot serve God and money.*
—MATTHEW 6:24

O F ALL THE cultures with access to excess, America is very likely the most excessive of all. As I have said for many years, our nation is rolling in excess, reveling in luxury, revolting in morals, and rotting in sin. If you need proof, just consider our national obsession with money. We are certainly not the only nation to idolize wealth, but we have done so to a degree heretofore unknown in the world.

While the Israelites were at Mount Sinai awaiting Moses' return from his conference with the Almighty, they became bored and distracted. Moses had disappeared into the cloud that covered the apex of the mountain. His encounter there with God lasted forty days. There was lightning and thunder, noises, clamor, and uproar like no person had ever heard before. The people presumed Moses must have perished. Something had to be done.

Someone looked back over their shoulder and surmised that they needed to go back to Egypt rather than continue their arduous journey into what they surely thought was an uncertain future. However, they would need to select a new leader, so the congregation persuaded Moses' brother, Aaron, to design a statue of a calf that he overlaid with gold. Gold was their idol in those days. Some things never change.

A major misconception regarding money is that it is evil. You can always find those around the church who will confidently affirm that even the Bible says so. Please allow my voice to be raised with even greater confidence to affirm that the Bible says no such thing. Here is what God's Word does say, from 1 Timothy 6:10: "For the love of money is the root of all evil. While coveting after money, some have strayed from the faith and pierced themselves through with many sorrows."

Money is not evil. It is neither good nor bad. It is simply a method of exchange developed to provide a method to acquire goods and services that are necessary or desirable. Money is simply a tool. Ask yourself this question: If money is inherently evil, why do people work forty hours a week or more to get it? The ways in which money can be used may be good or evil, but money itself is neutral. The love of money, however, is another matter entirely. As believers we have committed ourselves to loving God supremely. Anything we love more than or in place of God is an idol.

Another highly promoted and verifiably false myth is that the Bible condemns wealth. It does not—however, God's Word does condemn covetousness, defined as "excessive desire, especially for wealth or possessions."[1] I'm certain that you have encountered numerous individuals who are covetous despite the fact that they actually possess little or nothing. Wealth is not a vice, but it can very easily become a burden rather than a blessing. Wealthy people are not intrinsically evil. Some claim that the rich have only achieved wealth by unlawful or unethical means. Unfortunately, some have—and this is not just a relic of past generations. The well-documented and ongoing existence of child labor and sweatshops, illegal narcotics manufacturing, and human trafficking give ample testimony to the power and pervasiveness of the idol of covetousness.

Riches that are acquired by unlawful or unethical means are not a blessing to anyone—quite the opposite. King Midas, the protagonist in the ancient myth about the golden touch, discovered this to his dismay. He found that the ability to turn things into gold did not result in benefit. On the contrary, it destroyed everything that was precious to him.

I knew a man decades ago who confessed of his obsession with making money. He knew that his life would be complete if he could just make a thousand dollars per week—at that time it was a princely sum. He worked frantically and neglected weighty obligations in blind pursuit of his sole desire with single-minded, maniacal fervor. The day finally arrived when he had achieved his goal. Instead of being thrilled at his achievement, when he held that first one-thousand-dollar check in his hand, he wept like a child. His disappointment was unbounded because his idol—money—could never bring back to him all that he had lost in its pursuit.

The love of money has enticed hundreds of thousands to become involved in the nefarious world of transnational organized crime. According to the United Nations, the most lucrative illegal trades in the world are drug trafficking ($320 billion annually), human trafficking ($32 billion annually), migrant smuggling (estimated $7 billion annually), natural resource trafficking ($3.5 billion annually), sale of fraudulent medicines ($1.6 billion annually), and cybercrime ($1 billion annually). Other categories cannot be accurately measured, such as illegal firearms trading and the illegal trade of wildlife and wildlife parts.[2]

To say that these problems are only happening in undeveloped parts of the world is to close one's eyes and mind to the truth. The second-largest human trafficking ring in my home state of Ohio was operating within a few miles of the church it is my privilege to pastor. I am happy to report it is no longer in operation, in large part due to the efforts of intrepid people in our local church and the students of Valor Christian College who made it a priority to combat the plague with the love of God, the proclamation of the gospel of Christ, and prevailing prayer.

Listen to this graphic condemnation of the unrighteous among the wealthy, from James 5:1–6:

> Come now, you rich men, weep and howl for your miseries that shall come upon you. Your riches are corrupted and your garments are moth-eaten. Your gold and silver are corroded, and their corrosion will be a witness against you and will eat your flesh like fire. You have stored up treasures for the last days. Indeed the wages that you kept back by fraud from the laborers who harvested your fields are crying, and the cries of those who harvested have entered into the ears of the Lord of Hosts. You have lived in pleasure on the earth and have been wayward. You have nourished your hearts as in a day of slaughter. You have condemned and killed the righteous man who does not resist you.

Money is a good servant but a poor master. It will buy a house but will never produce a home. It can purchase sex but not love. It can acquire an alarm system, but it will be unable to provide security. It can purchase medicine but not health; a bed but not sleep. It can provide everything necessary from a material standpoint, but it can do absolutely nothing to provide for our spiritual needs.

However, it is wrong to assume that the only way to acquire an abundance of finances is by oppressing and victimizing others. There are many who have legitimately amassed great sums as a result of hard work, brilliant innovation, or creative activity.

Many times those who most stridently criticize wealthy individuals do so not because they truly care for the poor but because they are desperate to get their hands on a piece of the action for themselves. They are, in two words, covetous and jealous.

Just as we must never automatically condemn the rich, we must resist the temptation to hold poverty as a virtue. Those who exist in poverty do so for many reasons. Often, poverty rises to destroy people through no fault of their own. It may be the result of an accident or injury, poor health, natural disasters, or, yes, systemic oppression. In other cases, poverty has a direct correlation to the decisions individuals make. Possibilities range from a lack of restraint to irresponsible behavior or even criminal activity.

The point is, whether rich, poor, or somewhere in between, the love of money can be a problem for anyone, turning a useful and helpful means of exchange into a deceitful and demanding taskmaster. In fact, Colossians 3:5 lists covetousness last in a list of fleshly failures, and then plainly says it is idolatry.

Some maintain that the issue is that there is not enough wealth in the world. Organizations that track wealth agree that wealth is still being created world-wide—in fact, there is more of it than ever.[3] It is also true that no matter how much wealth is created, the disparity between those who have it and those who don't continues to increase.[4]

The reasons for this wealth gap as well as its answer are continuously debated. One train of thought is that wealth must be confiscated from the wealthy and be distributed to others. This proposal usually receives a lot of agreement from those affected most by poverty, but problems abound with this point of view. The greater problem becomes who decides how much gets taken and from whom, and who decides how much gets given and to whom.

Once again the Bible provides the solution to the entire issue. First Timothy 6:17–18 says, "Command those who are rich in this world that they not be conceited, nor trust in uncertain riches, but in the living God, who richly gives us all things to enjoy. Command that they do good, that they be rich in good works, generous, willing to share."

When those who possess the most wealth give generously to those who do not, it leaves third parties, such as governments or bureaucrats, out of the wealth redistribution equation. I might add that this generally irritates said third parties immeasurably, since they want to be the only ones to decide who gets what. Some who have achieved enormous wealth are extremely generous. Others, sadly, are not. They have to think of ways to spend their money, and it usually involves spending it on themselves or on their favorite people or pet causes.

A word now regarding gambling. Long considered an activity limited to the shady and seedy realm of the underworld, gambling is now legal in many places. Casinos, once found only in Las Vegas and a few other localities, have sprouted up across the country. Sports betting, including online betting, has been legalized by an increasing number of states and is gathering momentum. State-sponsored lotteries operate in all but a handful of states.

In the past, most people had to travel, often for long distances, to reach a gambling venue. Now bets can be placed online for nearly anything and from nearly anywhere. Lottery tickets can be purchased at retail stores in nearly every neighborhood. Americans love to spend money on the chance that they will hit it big. The vast majority of the time, all they hit is bottom. But that doesn't seem to diminish gambling's allure. The spirit of idolatry persuades people to do overtly foolish things— even as foolish as spending money that should be used for food or other essential household necessities—to fuel their addiction of thrill-seeking. In some cases, casual gambling matures quickly into a full-fledged addictive disorder that is equally damaging as a drug, alcohol, or sexual addiction.

Las Vegas remains without a doubt the gambling capital of the United States. The first casino was built there in 1906, and the first full-service hotel-casinos were built in the 1940s. They were small undertakings compared to today's hotels and casinos, which are enormous, world-class venues by any measure. One thing that has not changed is the gambling that takes place there. Commercial gaming revenue passed $60 billion for the first time in 2022, and 34 percent of adults in the US visited a casino over the course of the year.[5] People still travel to Las Vegas every year.

Gambling is a proposition for losers. The advantage for the casino varies depending upon the game played but may be anywhere from less than 1 percent to more than 40 percent. Less than 14 percent of gamblers come out winners in a casino.[6] I have heard described what is said to be the ultimate unforgettable traveling experience: flying the red-eye (an overnight flight) from Las Vegas in the middle seat of the coach section of a commercial airliner with a disappointed gambler who is overstuffed, broke, and intoxicated on either side of them. Viva Las Vegas indeed!

Playing state-sponsored lotteries may be considered harmless entertainment, but it is gambling. The odds for most games are among the longest of any type of gambling. Depending on the game and the number of tickets sold, the odds of drawing a single winning ticket in a multi-state lottery may be as high as 1 in 292 million.[7] (To give a sense of perspective, the odds of being struck by lightning is only 1 in 1.2 million.)[8] In addition, state-run lotteries only return about 60 percent of their income on prizes.[9] Most of the remainder is used for overhead and advertising, with a relatively small percentage going to government budgets. Americans spent over $105 billion on lottery tickets in 2021, and that money disproportionately came from lower-income households—the ones who can least afford that expense and loss.[10] Even in the unlikely event someone hits it big, consider this warning from Proverbs 13:11: "Wealth gained by vanity will be diminished, but he who gathers by labor will increase." I recommend you keep this in mind every time you hear about the next lottery winner. For every rags-to-riches story, there is another rags-to-riches-to-rags story as well.

This doesn't even begin to cover other forms of legalized gambling such as pari-mutuel betting (mostly horse racing), sports betting, and games of chance, all the way down to the weekly event at the local bingo hall.

Then, of course, there is illegal gambling, still in operation in the form of local bookmakers taking bets on anything imaginable. There are also the illegal numbers or policy rackets that may not be as widespread as they were a generation ago but are still in business in thousands of cities.

If there is anything that is a sure bet when it comes to gambling, it is this: the house always wins. Those winnings are in the form of money that comes from the pockets of the losers. In many cases, as I stated, the losers are those who can least afford the loss.

Speaking of losers, allow me to mention how greed and the lust for more money has contributed to some of the most shocking examples of fraudulent financial dealings in American history.

One of the most recent was the 2022 collapse of the

cryptocurrency exchange FTX. The majority stake-holders have been accused of living financed lavish life-styles while owing investors as much as $8 billion.[11]

Late in 2022, Wells Fargo bank was ordered to pay a $3.7 billion judgment due to the alleged mismanagement of as many as 16 million client accounts.[12]

Year after year, the energy company Enron was called one of America's most innovative companies by *Fortune* magazine. In mid-2000, its stock was trading at up to $90 a share. Only a few months later, its stock was trading for less than a dollar a share, majorly due to corporate and accounting malfeasance. The company declared bankruptcy in December 2001, valued at over $63 billion.[13]

In 1998, WorldCom merged with MCI Communications to become the second-largest telecommunications company in America. An internal audit led to the exposure of massive accounting irregularities as well as the resultant collapse of the company in 2002. The company had overstated its assets by $11 billion.[14]

In 2003, a Stanford student named Elizabeth Holmes dropped out of school to pursue her dream of opening Theranos, a health-care services company. The company was worth $10 billion in 2014. The next year, the company's automated blood testing device was declared unworkable. Theranos disintegrated in 2018, and its founder was sentenced to prison for conspiracy and wire fraud.[15]

In 2008, Bernard Madoff, the former head of NASDAQ and a stock market trader, was arrested and charged with fraud. He confessed to running what was essentially a gigantic Ponzi scheme that involved paying prior investors with the money entrusted to him by new investors. When his illegal enterprise crashed, investors lost as much as $65 billion, although that number has been disputed.[16] What is not disputed, however, is that the name Bernie Madoff is forever linked to fraud.

The examples I have cited are just a few of the most egregious examples of financial fraud that have made headlines in the recent past. Financial disasters large and small have been the legacy of grasping for more and more and more without any moral or ethical constraints. Money is designed to be used, but not to be trusted—and certainly not to be worshipped and idolized!

As I wrote in my book *Silent No More* all the way back in 2005, "We are swimming in a culture of debt. We are drowning in an unrestrained lust for more toys....The more we have, the more we want, and it is robbing us of peace, robbing us of community, and robbing us of any higher meaning for our lives. The things we demand and the debt we are willing to tolerate to have them are creating a bondage our children and our grandchildren will be forced to confront decades from now."[17]

When it comes to possessions and to debt, everything is bigger than it was a generation ago. Our vehicles are bigger. Our homes are bigger. Our beds are bigger. Our coffeepots and bath towels, our refrigerators and televisions are bigger. The debt we have acquired to accumulate all those things is bigger as well!

In 1949, a typical single-family home in the United States was 909 square feet. In 2021, that figure was 2,480 square feet.[18] Today, some homes have closets that are bigger than the bedrooms my sister and I occupied when we were children.

The median sale price of a single-family home in the US reached a peak of $420,900 in June of 2022. Since then, that figure has fallen to $412,300 as real estate values have declined some, mostly due to rising mortgage interest rates.[19]

Fifty years ago, in 1973, the median sale price of a single-family home was $27,698. Adjusted for inflation, that price would be $188,521 today.[20]

Let's say someone wants to purchase a $250,000 single-family home as their primary residence. They have a down payment of $10,000, making their loan amount $240,000. They qualify for a thirty-year fixed rate loan and a 6.5 percent interest rate. Their payment would be $1,517 per month, amounting to payments of $546,120 over the life of the loan. By that time, they will have paid the bank nearly 2.28 times the amount of money they borrowed. Can you see why the Bible shouts that "the borrower is servant to the lender" (Prov. 22:7)?

Credit card interest rates are now over 20 percent.[21] The average balance for credit card holders in December of 2022 was $7,279.[22] The average minimum payment on credit card balances more than a specified amount is often 2 percent of the balance.[23] If the cardholder only paid the minimum payment of their starting average balance of $7,279, or $145.58, it would take them just over 9 years (109 months) to pay off the balance, as long as no additional purchases were made in that time. In addition, the total interest paid ($8,502) would amount to more than the original balance.

Vehicles show the same sort of growth, in both size and expense. The most popular sedan in America, the Toyota Camry, is now 21 percent larger than when it was introduced. The most popular SUV, the Toyota RAV4, has a 34 percent size boost from its first design. The most popular pickup truck, the Ford F-150, is 25 percent bigger than its original counterpart.[24]

The average costs of these items are staggeringly higher than they were fifty years ago.

The most popular car sold in America in 1973 was the Chevrolet Monte Carlo, at a sticker price of $3,806—less than $20,000 in today's dollars. A 2023 Toyota Camry costs $27,315 today.

Here's a buying scenario that models what many thousands of borrowers experience when purchasing a new vehicle. At a $27,000 purchase price, a $1,000 down payment, and $2,300 in taxes, title, and fees, the total amount needing to be financed would be $28,300. A 60-month car loan at approximately 9 percent interest would involve payments of $540 per month, for a total cost of $32,400. In this example, $4,100 would go to the finance company as interest on the loan.

In addition, a vehicle will lose as much as 25 percent of its value by the beginning of the second year of ownership.[25] Chances are good that a buyer has not paid 25 percent of the vehicle's original value by that time. If an accident happens that results in the vehicle being a total loss, the buyer has what is known as negative equity. That is a fancy way of saying they owe more money to the bank or finance company than the vehicle is worth.

I'm not saying you should not purchase a home or vehicle. I am saying that debt is designed to keep you in financial bondage. We should not accept this as a normal condition that will never change as long as we live.

Debt has become the standard way of doing business for the federal government. The US national debt for fiscal year 2022 was $30.93 trillion—a number that is incomprehensible—and this debt continues to elevate and escalate with no end in sight.[26] We are truly a nation of borrowers and not owners.

Ancient moneylenders would look with envy at today's debt and interest rates. Whatever you purchase here on earth, regardless of how necessary it seems, is perishing. It will decay and diminish in value and importance over time. Eternal things, on the other hand, last forever.

Regarding borrowing, Proverbs 22:7 says very succinctly that "the rich rules over the poor, and the borrower is servant to the lender." One of the ways the borrower becomes a servant is that the lender makes the rules and the borrower must follow them. The borrower is in a subordinate position, and the lender is in the superior position. Ask anyone who has a mortgage if they own a home. They will almost invariably say they do. But who really owns the home? It is not the borrower—it is the lending institution to whom the mortgage is owed. If you doubt this, watch what happens when the borrower misses a few payments.

I know of at least two instances when banks foreclosed on churches even though no payments were in arrears. The bank took action based on the legal language of their contract regarding demographic and economic trends, and it did so with no apology or remorse. The borrowers had no recourse in these instances, and the church buildings were repossessed. The people who worshipped there had their lives disrupted. Indeed, the borrower is servant to the lender.

Here is another point to consider regarding borrowing money, and one that is often overlooked. An agreement to borrow money with interest is considered a contract. In legal terms, a contract can be seen as essentially the same as a covenant. (Spiritually speaking, a covenant may exceed the terms of a contract, but from a legal standpoint, the terms can be more or less equivalent.) Anyone who borrows with a mortgage or other legal debt instrument is in covenant with the lender. When people sign a contract or covenant to borrow money, they are joining themselves to a person or an organization whose background, spiritual condition, moral principles, or integrity is in most cases either unknown or unknowable.

Why is that a problem? It is this: 2 Corinthians 6:14 says, "Do not be unequally yoked together with unbelievers." I submit that believers who enter into a contract or covenant with lenders are, or at the very least could be, entering into a yoke of bondage with those who do not know or even acknowledge the God whom Christians serve. Shouldn't people be looking at other options instead of accepting debt as a way of life?

Here is another way to look at borrowing. Let's say you purchase an automobile that costs $30,000. (Many vehicles these days cost much more.) You enter into a contract to borrow money from a finance company to purchase the car. The entire cost of the loan will be much more than the purchase price due to interest. Let's say the total cost of the loan is $35,000. Let's also say your yearly salary is $70,000. What you have essentially done is signed away your life for six months to do nothing but pay for that loan.

I didn't say you would pay the loan off in six months. What I mean is that you have willingly devoted all your effort, labor, time, and energy to satisfy the terms of the loan. You have put yourself in bondage for six months of your life. Think of it as not being paid for six months—everything you make will go to the finance company. In the meantime, your other obligations continue as they always do. How will you pay your other bills during that time? You are in servitude to the lender. They own you for six months. You can't make decisions about what you are going to do with your money during that time—that decision has already been made. Is that car worth six months of your life?

First Timothy 6:7 makes a bold, matter-of-fact statement: "For we brought nothing into this world, and it is certain that we can carry nothing out."

Perhaps that is the reason why so many people attempt to carry as much stuff and as many things with them during this lifetime as possible. Placing more value on temporal things than on eternal ones is a primary and principal form of blatant idolatry in America. May God Almighty deliver us!

# Chapter 8

# OFF ITS AXIS: THE PREEMINENCE OF EARTH, NATURE, AND THE UNIVERSE

*The universe is all that is or was or ever will be.*
—CARL SAGAN, 1980, *COSMOS: A PERSONAL VOYAGE*

*They turned the truth of God into a lie and worshipped and served the creature rather than the Creator, who is blessed forever. Amen.*
—ROMANS 1:25

THOSE WHO LIVE in urban areas where light pollution spills into the sky and obscures the view of the stars are at a disadvantage. However, even a limited view of the night sky will fill all but the most unimaginative of souls with a sense of awe and wonder.

This immensity was in view when God encouraged Abram to step outside his tent and observe the stars

(Gen. 15:5). David had the same thing in mind when he wrote Psalm 8:3–4: "When I consider Your heavens, the work of Your fingers, the moon and the stars, which You have established, what is man that You are mindful of him, and the son of man that You attend to him?"

There are basically two directions of philosophical thought when considering the heavens as the patriarch and the psalmist did. On one hand, a person can regard the starry hosts as the handiwork of God and be inspired to ascribe reverence to Him because of the magnificence of His creation. On the other, a person may choose to worship the creation itself rather than the Creator.

It has been my privilege to be outdoors long before daybreak on many occasions. When the skies are clear in the very early hours, I revel in the knowledge that a good and gracious God alone created everything that I see—and even more that I cannot see from my vantage point on the earth.

On the other hand, there are many in our postmodern and post-Christian world who do not use their observations of the heavens as an opportunity to worship the Creator of it all. Alternately, they worship the actual heavens themselves—and by extension, everything that belongs to the cosmos, including the earth. Many who ascribe to this ideology also regard humans as either predators, parasites, or a plague, whose rapacious inclinations must be held in abeyance lest man destroy his only home. According to adherents of this doctrine, we are well on our way to doing exactly that.

In these matters, I cannot ignore or dismiss the devastating trends that are occurring in the environment. I am not unaware of the dilemma that exists between the need for economic opportunity and development and the need to preserve a safe and sustainable habitat and home planet.

For generations my family was involved in the coal mining industry, which has traditionally been a risky endeavor not only in terms of personal safety but also in terms of danger to the environment. The mines were a significant source of energy production and the economic engine of entire regions. However, there are streams not far from my home that are perpetually stained orange and nearly devoid of life because of polluted water seeping out of mines that were abandoned after coal production ceased.

I don't believe we should advocate resource extraction or any other kind of industry without appropriate environmental safeguards. Neither do I think we should automatically ban everything that could potentially pose a risk to anything in the environment. To do so places people at unnecessary risk and makes the environment an idol—more important than any other consideration.

There are an abundance of potential conflicts in this area. For instance, I think people should have the freedom to build a house on their property where it suits them. I understand the need for zoning laws that protect us from someone raising up a building right next to a neighboring home or blocking the view from an intersection. However, I must warn against zoning regulations that are so extreme that they prevent a dwelling from being built just about anywhere.

Any type of development, whether it is a high-rise building in a downtown metropolis or a backyard fire pit, creates some form of consequence for the environment. If we don't build anything, the animals and plants won't be disturbed. Yet if we shut it all down, people's lives will be disrupted and ultimately diminished.

Fellow citizens may enjoy the backyard vista of a sunset on the ocean, or want to live at the edge of a watercourse to take advantage of the recreational opportunities it affords. In my opinion they should have liberty to do so as long as they understand that the risk they are taking is theirs alone. If a hurricane or flood devastates their property, they should not seek relief by demanding some form of government subsidy or bail-out. In addition, economic loss due to a natural disaster should not be an opportunity for certain groups to claim that the event was due to some climate trend that may not have had anything to do with the outcome.

Habitat loss is particularly problematic for people like me who enjoy pursuing wild game. Every parking lot, housing development, and warehouse that springs up supplants the wildlife that called that space home. But in spite of how much I enjoy seeing rabbits and raccoons, I refuse to oppose the jobs, homes, and other opportunities that those developments make available. God made the earth for a particular purpose, as Isaiah 45:18 makes clear: "For thus says the LORD, who created the heavens, who is God, who formed the earth and made it, who has established it, who did not create it in vain, who formed it to be inhabited: I am the LORD, and there is no other."

God intends for humans to make wise use of the earth He created for us. We must not forget that it is human beings, not animals, who are the ultimate beneficiaries of God's creative activity. This is by His design, not by some happy accident of evolution or some other theory devised by men.

I am no perpetual pessimist claiming that we are all going to die if we don't stop drinking the water and breathing the air. I will agree to ban plastic drinking straws as soon as someone can develop an alternative that won't disintegrate before I am finished attempting to extract my beverage from the plastic container in which the plastic straw banner served my drinks to me.

I am irritated by litter, and by those who carelessly throw their refuse where someone else will have to deal with it. I try to set a good example at home and at work by picking up trash when I see it, and I encourage others to do the same. The front lawn or the church parking area should not look like a dumping ground for everyone passing by.

I am in favor of recycling initiatives, and I understand there is a fortune in reusable materials lying in roadside ditches throughout the country. If we just recycled the aluminum cans that are thrown from automobiles onto the sides of the nation's roads, we could substantially reduce the amount of bauxite mined to make aluminum.

I am not, however, in favor of recycling mandates that make everyone conform to a certain standard of behavior, especially when those mandates are not economically viable.

It is part of our responsibility as believers to steward the earth's resources in a way that is ethical and sustainable. I don't want to see any part of God's creation exploited in such a way that it would poison the soil, air, and water, endanger wildlife, or irrevocably harm other natural resources. I will advocate on behalf of protecting and preserving historically and culturally significant sites and wilderness vistas for future generations to enjoy. I believe that these positions are appropriate for a believer in the God who created it all and who affords each of us the opportunity to steward it.

What I don't believe is appropriate is to worship the creation rather than the Creator, which is exactly what it appears some activists are attempting to do. If they would limit their worship to their personal convictions and devotions, that would not be much of a problem. However, as you may have noticed, they don't and won't stop there. They use all the resources at their disposal to try to convince everyone that their position is the only legitimate one, even going so far as attempting to manipulate data to confirm their beliefs and biases. In extreme cases, if they can't convince others by appealing to facts or reasoning, they apply pressure and shaming tactics to coerce them by applying the force of economic or regulatory mechanisms.

Perhaps no area of this conflict reveals earth worship

greater than the matter of what was once called "global warming" and is now referred to by the more generic term "climate change."

Is the climate changing? Of course it is! One of the best-known Christmas songs in America is "White Christmas." When I was young, Christmas Day involved snow-covered vistas everywhere in the American Midwest. Now, the first snow that remains often does not occur until mid-January. Just from an anecdotal standpoint, we can see that the climate is changing.

This should come as no surprise because we live in a dynamic world, not a static one. Although the motion of the planets is well regulated, there are deviations and shifts that are normal in any system as vast as the one in which we all live. For instance, the Medieval Warm Period was an approximately three-hundred-year time span between the years 950 and 1250 in which temperatures, at least in the northern hemisphere, were warmer than usual. It was followed by what is known as the Little Ice Age, which lasted from the sixteenth century to the nineteenth century. During the Medieval Warm Period, glaciers in Europe melted. During the Little Ice Age, rivers in middle America froze solid enough to allow regular activity upon and across them.[1]

To admit that change is occurring should not threaten anyone. Change is a fact of life, and managing change is an important life skill. The questions regarding climate change that generate the most controversy are these:

◊ What is causing climate change?

◊ What needs to be done about the change
   that is occurring?

These questions and their potential answers have
become some of the most contentious issues of our time.
One principle we must not forget in this discussion is
that God arranged for the seasons and the inevitable
changes they bring. Genesis 8:22 says, "While the earth
remains, seedtime and harvest, cold and heat, summer
and winter, and day and night will not cease." In addition, those dismayed by the alarming reports that seem
to occur on a daily basis will do well to remember what
Psalm 24:1 says: "The earth belongs to the LORD, and
its fullness, the world, and those who dwell in it." God
is the ultimate owner of everything. Although man may
not have been the responsible steward of the earth and
its resources that God would have preferred, the final
disposition of the world belongs to Him and not to us.

The end of the world will not be prompted by men's
activity but according to God's timeline. When this
world has finally fulfilled its purpose, God will create
a new one. Revelation 21:1 says, "Then I saw 'a new
heaven and a new earth.' For the first heaven and the
first earth had passed away, and there was no more
sea." We would do well to allow more of a heavenly
perspective to inform our earthly decisions, attitudes,
and actions.

There are those who maintain that climate change
depends upon human activity. This is called anthropo-
genic global warming, or AGW. This view states that
increased human population and activity, especially the

use of fossil fuels and the attendant release of carbon dioxide into the atmosphere, is causing global warming.

The reasoning of those holding this view is that since human activity is the cause of global warming, human activity must be altered in order to prevent it, or at least slow it down. This is where some of the most strident conflicts regarding this subject occur. And no wonder, since most of the policy prescriptions involving global warming demand restrictions and regulations that directly curtail freedoms, interfere with personal liberty, and ultimately have a very negative economic impact for individuals and nations.

Becoming involved in all the details of the climate change controversy is a task far exceeding my scope here. Rather, what I intend to show is that extreme positions regarding man's influence on climate change lead to some radical propositions. Some of those theories involve regarding the earth as an idol to be esteemed with greater value than the humans who inhabit it. The end result of those positions seems like more of an effort to control fellow human beings than to save the planet.

One example is the increase in carbon dioxide in the atmosphere. Conventional wisdom (which is often neither wise nor conventional) has concluded that this is a significant cause of climate change. According to this view, if the earth's temperatures continue to increase, disaster will surely occur, including rising ocean levels, agricultural implosion, water shortages, and more. Since these disasters will occur if something is not done, people need to change their behaviors to reduce the amount of carbon dioxide released into the atmosphere. This can be done by eliminating all sources of carbon dioxide emissions, such as fossil fuel–burning power plants, automobiles, industrial discharges—and yes, even farm animals.

These recommendations are not someday, pie-in-the-sky dreams; they are at this moment becoming translated into policy prescriptions far and wide. What this means in practical terms is that you and I will be required to pay much more for heating and cooling; we will have to either purchase electric vehicles or not drive; and we will also not have the number, variety, or availability of products that we now enjoy. In more extreme versions of the idolatrous climate cult, we will no longer eat meat, and everyone will live in cities and use public transportation exclusively.

Those who argue for these outcomes hysterically shout that it is the only way to rescue our home planet from soon and certain destruction. Those who resist such eventualities say that it would do little good to save a planet on which we would all have to go back to living in miserable conditions.

A particularly contentious problem that arises with the green agenda is the information (or misinformation, or disinformation) that has accompanied some of the pronouncements of its promoters. Predictions have been repeated endlessly, with attendant demands for immediate change. When the prediction becomes manifestly untrue, the proponents do not admit that they were wrong and their prognostications completely inaccurate—they simply make a new prediction with a different timeline.

Another tactic of those faithful to green worship is the use of words that cannot be accurately quantified, such as *near future* and *significant.* What these words mean differs depending on who is using them or hearing them. When a prediction does not come true, the predictor claims they didn't mean what you thought they meant.

Yet another scheme is to make some claims that are almost sure to be true and then use those to bolster their credentials for the reliability of their next prophecy, which may or may not prove to be accurate. It's no wonder the prophets of climate doom have an extensive credibility problem.

Other well-publicized controversies occurred when one group of scientists published data that they said supported their claims, but when other scientists analyzed the data, they either disagreed with it or could not reproduce it. There is disagreement in the scientific community regarding nearly everything. That is a part of the scientific process, which involves developing a hypothesis and then testing it or gathering data to see whether it is valid or not. It appears that regarding climate change, some people begin with certain conclusions and then seek to accumulate information that reinforces their predetermined conclusions. That is not a recipe for effective persuasion—especially when you are attempting to persuade people to pay more, sacrifice more, eat less, and have less.

One statement that climate activists have made endlessly in order to convince people and governments to fall in line with their agenda is that 97 percent of climate scientists agree about climate change. In addition to being extremely unlikely, that statistic is simply not factual.[2]

Why would people want to promote ideas about outcomes that may not happen? In the case of climate change, it is impossible to make reliable predictions because no one can state with any degree of certainty how one degree of average temperature change will affect sea levels or desert sizes. I have several suggestions about why this happens so frequently.

I was interviewed on a national news program about the controversy regarding stem cell research. The host said that the scientists researching the potential of stem cells said it showed great promise. Of course they would say that. What researcher worth their degree would say his or her line of research showed no promise? That is certainly no way to attract grant money to conduct additional research. To say that such bias cannot exist in the scientific community is to say that scientists are not human.

In addition, academics who refuse to agree with the accepted narrative are subjected to varying types of pressure to conform. Their pathways to promotion may be blocked, or they may not receive the same opportunities offered to others unless they repeat the accepted mantras.

Organizations that are invested in the prevailing

narrative receive contributions based on how desperate they can make the situation appear. The more alarming the news (or the press releases), the more likely it is that they will be able to draw support from those who show interest in their cause.

Politicians and policymakers may feel the need to take some sort of immediate action to give the impression that they are doing something about the emergency to gain favor with their constituents. Businesses that are invested in the narrative may feel pressure to advance the hyperbole so that their products or services will continue to be in demand.[3]

The climate change controversy is in no way the only indicator of exalting the creation over its Creator. The so-called Green Agenda has other issues it will be happy to share with you, but with which it will also seek your conformity. The Green New Deal proposed in 2019 seeks to implement policies that would make America reach net-zero emissions by 2030,[4] meaning the country would not emit more atmospheric gases than it removed.

Among the proposals in the Green New Deal is a commitment to clean and renewable energy sources such as wind and solar power, as well as the elimination of coal and natural gas as energy sources. The problems attending this proposal are enormous. For instance, the wind doesn't always blow, and the sun doesn't always shine; therefore, any energy infrastructure dependent upon those sources is inherently unreliable.

Another feature of the Green New Deal is an emphasis

on electric vehicles. A great advantage of electric vehicles is that they are clean, at least in terms of carbon emissions. A huge disadvantage of electric vehicles, however, is that they have to be recharged at recharging stations. And exactly from where does the power to recharge them flow? Well, of course it comes from the electric grid, which would presumably be powered by the same unreliable wind and solar inputs.

The Green New Deal promotes public transportation and high-speed rail. In order for those options to work, those modes of transportation will need to take people anywhere they need or want to go. In terms of high-speed rail, California is presently experimenting and is having a hard time delivering on the promises of building a high-speed train from Los Angeles to San Francisco.[5]

All of these policy proposals and their associated costs have prompted critics to ask: Is this about saving the planet or is it about centralized control of the economy and its inevitable corollary—the control of people? If people control is the real issue, the worship of the planet is only a ruse to gain approval for policies that would continue or accelerate the erosion of individual freedoms.

There is one more category of earth worship I want to address, and that is extreme animal rights activists. I'm not referring to the cat lady who lives in your neighborhood or the friend who has chosen a vegan diet for personal reasons. I'm talking about those who go so far as to say you should never again own a pet, since that is exploiting animals, or you should never again eat meat, since an animal will have to die in order to make that a possibility.[6]

Humane treatment of animals is a biblical principle. (See Proverbs 12:10.) We should never allow or contribute to animal abuse or mistreatment—and that has been far too widespread in our country. However, valuing animals and treating them humanely is far different from giving them equal status to humans. The only things created by God in His image are human beings. Animals, including fish and birds, are wonderful creatures, but they do not have the same unique characteristics or status as people.

A small but growing (in both numbers and influence) group of animal rights activists disagree. In extreme cases, they threaten violence against those they perceive are exploiting animals, including sportsmen, breeders, and medical researchers. One group has a history of releasing animals kept in pens, such as at fur farms. Ironically, some of the animals they release die due to stress, being struck by vehicles, or conflict with other animals. In these cases, the activists' efforts to relieve what they perceive as suffering results in more suffering.[7]

In a more recent development, scientists appear to have found evidence that plants let out ultrasonic sounds when they are stressed.[8] I suppose it is only a matter of time before someone will recommend we not eat plants because of the pain humans cause them. (Screaming tomatoes, anyone? That sounds to me like a great name for an alternative rock band.)

Well-meaning individuals can disagree on the virtues or values of certain actions and decisions, such as what forms of recreation to have, what to wear, or what to eat. However, when these actions or decisions are the result of valuing the earth, the universe, or animals more highly than their Creator or the human race that He created in His own image, it is not called justice, compassion, tolerance, or equity. It is idolatry.

## Chapter 9

# ABOVE ALL: COMFORT, CONVENIENCE, SAFETY, AND SECURITY

*A ship in harbor is safe, but that is not what ships are built for.*
—JOHN AUGUSTUS SHEDD, 1928, *SALT FROM MY ATTIC*

*For where your treasure is, there will your heart be also.*
—MATTHEW 6:21

WHEN I WAS a child, amusement parks were not the big business they are today. We actually were required to find ways to entertain ourselves that were free, or at least inexpensive. When we would visit home, in eastern Kentucky, I would spend more hours than I can remember searching for those special places where wild grapevines grew in profusion among the hardwood trees.

The ideal grapevine was one that grew in such a way

that we could swing on it to the other side of a ravine or across a swimming hole. The vine had to be large enough to support our weight but small enough that we could wrap our child-sized hands around it. We would cut one close to the ground with our trusty pocketknife (no easy task) and do our best Tarzan imitation as we swung on the vine until one of two things inevitably occurred: either our arms became too weary to hold on, or the vine would break from the constant stress.

The fear of falling only heightened our excitement of swinging far above the ground in what to us was a grav-ity-defying stunt. It was a far cry from the g-forces gener-ated by today's mega-coasters at modern amusement parks, but for us it was fantastic entertainment. I carry memories of those times as trophies of days well spent.

We learned a valuable life lesson. There is risk that accompanies every reward. Although death or dismem-berment was unlikely, there still abided the unmistak-able thrill of the fleeting thought of plummeting onto the rocks that always seemed to be lurking under the ideal grapevines. Somehow, we managed to survive.

Bumps and bruises, blisters and bee stings, stubbed toes, scraped knees, and sunburns were all standard representations of the joys of boyhood. As kids, we just regarded them as a low price to pay for having fun and enjoying life.

At times more serious accidents did occur. One such mishap resulted in a compound fracture to my left fore-arm when I was eight years old. It happened at the beginning of summer, and my arm from shoulder to mid-fingers was encased in a plaster cast for six weeks. I taped a plastic bag over it and went swimming anyway. I counted the days until I could get back to my usual activities without being burdened by that mass of plaster keeping me from my obligations—who, after all, was going to keep the peace as only I could in the raucous western town that was our suburban backyard? Why, I couldn't draw my left six-shooter cap pistol with my arm in a cast. We were sure to be overrun by outlaws! I just couldn't understand my mother's solicitous oversight, or her concern when I did things that put myself at what she must have thought was unnecessary risk.

Two things happened that changed my point of view. One was that I grew up, and I began to realize that injuries were actually no laughing matter and could have serious and long-lasting consequences. The other is that I got married and had children of my own. I suddenly had a judicious concern for the well-being of my offspring that exceeded any thought I'd had for my own safety when I was a kid. I was surpassed in this regard only by my wife, Joni.

As our children grew, Joni and I wanted them to experience as many opportunities and activities as we could offer them. One of the first things we provided was a typical swing set. We were sure that it was a benign blessing that would afford the children a chance to do something they enjoyed in the relative safety of our backyard.

They enjoyed it, sure enough. Not only that, but as a result of their prepubescent ingenuity, they developed methods of use we'd never imagined. I distinctly remember hearing our daughter Ashton at six years old calling to us from outside of the house. I thought she was enjoying the swing set. She was, indeed; however, not in the conventional way of sitting in a swing. Nope. She was walking barefoot across the top bar of the apparatus as though it was a balance beam. I rushed out to the swings as nonchalantly as possible, as I didn't want to cause her to lose her concentration, slip, and fall. My sense of relief when she leaped into my trembling arms was as tangible as the event was memorable. If you can't abide risks, my best advice is that you never attempt parenting.

The risk-and-reward conundrum illustrates one of the dilemmas, and some might say one of the mysteries, of the human condition. We may fear risk, and yet we are attracted to it, even fascinated by it. How else can popular activities be explained? The masses seek the adrenaline rush of inherently risky adventures like base and bungee jumping, parachuting, motorcycle racing, mountain climbing, and transoceanic sailing.

What about the risks involved in gambling (including purchasing lottery tickets) or, for that matter, a friendly game of backgammon or bridge? Let me take it a step further and include financial investing as a nexus of the risk/reward relationship. Every financial advisor will maintain that there are risks involved with every reward. We may enjoy the temporary thrill of risk taking, but we seek safety. If we are realistic, we come to realize we can never create nor find anywhere on earth a 100 percent safe environment.

That begs a question: Where are you ever truly and completely safe? In a movie theater? At a marathon? A ticketed concert? Walking down the sidewalk? Going to school or to church? In your vehicle? Recent headlines confirm that none of these places can guarantee or even assure safety. If the threat of violence isn't enough to give you pause about venturing out, consider the recent pandemic and remember a terrified populace sequestering themselves inside their homes and suspecting everyone they encountered of being a potential vector of a deadly contagion. Sadly, for some, the trauma of COVID-19 has made many such changes in behavior permanent.

All of these factors have conspired to cause people to become exceedingly defensive and afraid—far beyond normalcy. I believe what we are witnessing is the result of something taking place below the surface and behind the scenes, something of more than simply human origin. Allow me to explain.

The second of the three pillars of a distinctively Christian worldview is the one about which people have the most questions. It perhaps generates more controversy than the other two combined. (I give a thorough explanation of the concept of worldview in my book *Culturally Incorrect.*) It answers a vast array of questions concerning why terrible, even tragically bad things happen. Here it is in its sublime simplicity: we live in a fallen world. And as Romans 5:12 explains, the effects of the fall involve all of those who dwell on this planet: "Therefore as sin came into the world through one man and death through sin, so death has spread to all men, because all have sinned."

In the genesis of God's creation there was but a singular risk, one that God created in man. It was this: God so valued freedom that He gave mankind free moral agency. Adam had the God-given gift and ability to choose. As we know, he made a wrong choice and wound his moral clock backward. He sided with God's great archenemy, Satan, and swung open the door for death, disease, decay, and destruction to enter the earth and human experience. We have been plagued by the effects of the disobedient choice of our pristine parents in the garden and the subsequent fall ever since.

Humans have a built-in desire to preserve our lives— to seek safety. Yet we also have a built-in desire to express ourselves, to create, and to experience freedom from the constraints that staying safe so often demands. How do we square this circle?

The prevailing impulse appears to be to demand safety for ourselves, regardless of the cost. We seem to have forgotten that everyone possesses the same free moral agency that Adam did; that is, we can make choices, and choices have consequences.

There is no doubt that safety should be an important consideration in every situation and station in life. There is also no doubt that we have made great progress in this area over the past generations or even decades. We must also realize that there are certain occupations that are inherently dangerous, and no amount of safety features or training will eliminate all risks. Industries such as logging, commercial fishing, farming, mining, energy production, construction, law enforcement, firefighting, and a host of others are consistently more dangerous than others. Where would we be without the brave men and women who take those risks and expose themselves to great dangers?

Who can forget the image of eleven workmen on a tall building sitting on an exposed steel beam eating their lunch with no harnesses or other safety features in sight?[1] Or of high scalers rappelling down the cliffs adjacent to the location of the Hoover Dam with only rudimentary harnesses and ropes to hold them?[2] How about the worker standing on scaffolding giving the Statue of Liberty a kiss on the forehead during its renovation?[3]

Physical safety is certainly not the greatest problem these days. Lately our culture has been flooded with demands for emotional safety. One of the issues is bullying in schools. No child should feel unsafe while either at school or on their way to and from school. Harassment, intimidation, and shaming is never acceptable, especially when directed toward our youngest and most vulnerable.

A larger problem, however, may be those children who never grow up and who demand safety even from opposing viewpoints. In fact, even the possibility of being exposed to a differing opinion becomes so triggering and debilitating that going to work or school is beyond the realm of feasibility. All of this has created a flood of excesses in our homes and churches as well as on college campuses, in the workplace, and in the marketplace. These changes have taken place with stunning swiftness.

Casual comments here become microaggressions. Course content must be preceded by trigger warnings. Guest speakers are disinvited or shouted down because their position or topic is not one that is preferred by some segment of the student body. They may be banned because of remarks they made or actions they took decades ago, regardless of whether or not one's past reflects their current thinking.

College campuses become preservation pods for emotional adolescents as opposed to institutions that emphasize the robust exchange of concepts and ideas. Students are not in command of the facts but are very much in tune with their feelings. In much of the culture, feelings matter much more than facts. Heaven forbid they would ever have to confront a set of principles or arguments that differ from those to which they cling with such fear and blinded ferocious tenacity. Their delicate sensibilities are much too fragile to ever be confronted with differing opinions, much less facts. Their pitiful cry is, "Please don't confuse us with the facts. It's just too overwhelming."

The mantra of the nation's new flower children, "That offends me!" has become a default emotional setting for response to anything uncomfortable. Make no mistake; the prevailing attitude is that if they are offended, they must be protected at any cost. The problem is that they are offended by everything, including any point of view that is divergent from their own. The tyranny of the few is thereby displayed in all its multidimensional splendor. Debate or even discussion of ideas grinds to a halt because of the fear of verbal, emotional, physical, or even violent retribution.

These emotionally stunted and pampered children masquerading as adults have in many cases been steeped in a culture that has afforded them every advantage and catered to their every whim, allowing them to demand their perceived rights while forsaking their legitimate responsibilities.

The seedbed of this behavior must be laid at the feet of excessively indulgent parents convinced that their children are incapable of doing anything wrong. Such individuals will seize upon every opportunity to turn the slightest indiscretion into a four-alarm emergency, with their child always portrayed as the innocent victim. Mom, Dad, I have news for you: those protuberances on your child's back are shoulder blades, not angel's wings. When children of the Greatest Generation were disciplined at school, they knew such discipline would be supported by Dad and Mom when they got home and met with a double dose of the same.

Entitlement mentality expresses itself in multiple areas. First of all, it manifests in disrespect for oneself and for all authority figures and symbols. In the classroom it is apparent in lack of attendance as well as not paying attention in classes. Why should students apply themselves if they are going to pass the course regardless of their amount of effort? Ask any student who is concerned with their level of performance what it is like to be assigned to a study group with one of these slackers—or more than one. They end up doing their work and the entitled loafers' work as well.

This attitude has also become common in the workplace. If you can get them off the sofa, out of the basement, or away from the video game controller, entitled individuals show up late, leave early, and think of ways to do as little as possible while they are there. Their sensitivity is as high as their productivity is low. However, they are extremely proficient at fault-finding and complaining—about their low income and long hours. Then it's the inconvenient schedule, the uncomfortable working conditions, their repressive responsibilities, their coworkers, their supervisors, and anything and everything else. And then they have the audacity to wail in disbelief when no one chooses them to be on their team. They are worshipping at the idolatrous altar of self. They are self-willed, self-indulgent, self-satisfied, self-everything except self-sacrificing.

If entitled people can't get their way themselves, they can always find a sympathetic attorney to sue an imaginary offender on their behalf. We have lived in a litigious society for some time, but so-called lawfare suits have now become the order of the day. *Lawfare* is defined in Wikipedia as "the use of legal systems and institutions to damage or delegitimize an opponent, or to deter [an] individual's usage of their legal rights."[4] These legal actions are taken to stifle dissent, delegitimize opponents, or to gain a financial windfall from a person or corporation who would rather settle a suit—even one without merit—than to become involved in expensive litigation or public scrutiny.

Another alarming development is that entitled people will turn to educational, governmental, or business entities or nonprofit groups to provide them with protection against harm. Protection is what those suffering from delusional entitlement seek for themselves—however, they are quick to recommend persecution or cancellation of others, especially those with opposing views. The organizations involved can employ tactics that are frighteningly akin to those of totalitarian regimes. These include not allowing dissent, stifling free speech, political persecution, violating civil rights, physical violence, destruction of property, theft, and accusing and even jailing those who have conflicting viewpoints.

These developments in no way point to progress. We are going in reverse at warp speed rather than moving cautiously forward, and all in the name of the twin idols of safety and security.

No nation on earth has attained the level of material and financial security that we have enjoyed in the United States of America. You would think we would be the most grateful nation in the world. Unfortunately, you would be wrong. Greed, rather than gratitude, has become the fundamental motivating principle for a countless multitude. Americans are intoxicated with "things," and they love their stuff. Our neighbors will do anything to acquire more possessions and property, personal effects and paraphernalia, clothing, cars, trucks and trailers, thingamajigs and thingamabobs, doohickies and doodads, whether they need them or not. This is nothing more than idolatry. It may not involve kneeling down to a statue, but it is equally idolatrous in God's eyes. I pray that you are beginning to glimpse the ocean of idolatry in which we are awash.

I am not suggesting that we retreat to the Stone Age and return to cooking over open fire and living in caves. I suppose I enjoy the comforts of indoor plumbing and central heating and air-conditioning as much as anyone does. I certainly remember summer nights as a child, lying in bed near an open window, trying to go to sleep while listening to a rotary fan and the buzzing of mosquitoes searching for a landing spot on my tender skin. I recall visiting relatives' homes in the hills of Kentucky where the only bathroom was outside and rain barrels sufficed for plumbing. There were a couple of advantages: the plumbing never clogged, and during cold weather, bathroom visits were brief. But I suppose the greatest benefit was that I became grateful for what we had when we got back home. Gratefulness is the best antidote I know for entitlement.

Again, I'm not advocating that we return to such meager conditions, but neither do I want to condone the conspicuous consumerism that has captured so many in this nation. Here's a sobering thought for this snowflake generation: according to the 2023 U.N. World Water Report, 26 percent of the world's population, or two billion people, have no access to safe drinking water and 46 percent, or 3.6 billion people, have no access to sanitization.[5] I'm sure they would all rejoice to have my relatives' facilities and barrels of clean rainwater today!

Americans don't just desire or dream of their creature comforts—they *demand* them. Advertisers are more than happy to fuel this obsession, and corporations are gleefully doing their best to keep up with the demand. When our homes overflow with more things, we just rent storage units and fill them up with whatever won't fit. Garages are no longer used for vehicle storage, since they are full of boxes and bags and stacks and shelves of items that don't have a home anywhere else. Everyone seems to lament that they have too much stuff while stalking the stalls of flea markets and scouring the tables at yard sales, looking for the next bargain. Here is a secret my father taught us—it's not a bargain if you don't need it, regardless of how low the cost!

Not only is the drive to acquire more stuff incessant, but whatever "it" is must be possessed with immediacy. Online shopping is an exploding phenomenon—so convenient, so easy, so effortless! Not only that, someone in a uniform in a truck with a log delivers it right to your door! If people can't receive something right away, they are unwilling to wait. In the words of one of my high school coaches, we want it immediately, if not sooner.

In addition to all this, it is paramount that our purchases be convenient but also comfortable. From chairs to mattresses to automobile seats to clothing to lawnmowers to you name it, comfort has become the principal concern. I don't advocate that we all wear shirts made from camel's hair to prove our dedication to denial or to score some points on the ascetic scale. If someone wants to wear shoes that are comfortable rather than fashionable, I say more power to them. As Joni often remarks, "Beauty is pain."

However, I have observed those who will go to any length to avoid even the slightest discomfort, regardless of how necessary it may be—such as working, thinking, or even responding to a text in a timely manner. As a people we have become accustomed to staying in our sleepwear while sitting on our sofas with two different drinks, a snack, and a remote control close at hand. Oh, I forgot—your smart TV is probably equipped with voice activation, so you won't even need to push a button. Bless your weary heart! We reject anything that requires more effort than the bare minimum as an unnecessary and intrusive inconvenience.

A previous generation had a word to describe such a person. It was not *unmotivated, tired, overworked, distracted,* or *offended*—it was *lazy.* In every age there have been those who have done their level best to avoid work of any kind. I've observed those who actually work harder at not working than they would to just do their assignment. It surely becomes tiring to work at one's play and play at one's work.

There was a time, before political correctness was required, that those individuals who were able but refused to work or be productive members of society were referred to as loafers, layabouts, deadbeats, shirkers, and other unprintable appellations. Today it is likely that the non-contributers will be celebrated for their hostility toward honest labor instead of being called out for refusing to do anything to move any cause forward—any cause, that is, except for their own convenience and comfort.

I have probably noticed this most in church attendance. When restrictions due to the recent pandemic caused churches to close, they had to adapt. Many churches began offering their services by means of online streaming. The technology that was already available enabled tens of thousands of houses of worship to continue sending worship and prayer, preaching and teaching, children's services and ministry content of all kinds directly into homes so people could continue to be nurtured spiritually in a time of national crisis.

When the worst of the emergency was over and churches once again opened their doors, far too many who had become accustomed to watching church at their convenience never returned to in-person services. After all, they didn't have to get up, get ready, get the children fed and dressed, drive some distance, see other folks, interact with possible strangers, and so on. They could stay in their pajamas and sip their morning coffee while kicking back and putting their feet up. In the meantime, they lost the communion of the saints—the fellowship of believers. The church of Jesus Christ is quite diminished in its ability to minister to them, their families, and a hurting world because of their absence. You have probably heard it before, but I need to remind you that Hebrews 10:25 still says, "Let us not forsake the assembling of ourselves together, as is the manner of some, but let us exhort one another, especially as you see the Day approaching."

We are truly in a crisis of comfort in America and in the church. May God awaken us from our slumber at ease in Zion. Leonard Ravenhill said it this way:

> Could a mariner sit idle if he heard the drowning cry? Could a doctor sit in comfort and just let his patients die? Could a fireman sit idle, let men burn and give no hand? Can you sit at ease in Zion with the world around you damned?[6]

Comfort, convenience, safety, and security—all of them are desirable, but they are not the most important things in our lives. They have become idols one and all. May we destroy these idols as Gideon destroyed the altars of Baal and cut down the unholy Asherah poles. (See Judges 6.)

# Chapter 10

# FRACTURED FOUNDATION: FAMILY

*I used to think that the worst thing in life was to end
up all alone. It's not. The worst thing in life is ending
up with people who make you feel all alone.*
—Bobcat Goldthwait, 2009, *World's Greatest Dad*

*He who loves father or mother more than Me
is not worthy of Me. And he who loves son or
daughter more than Me is not worthy of Me.*
—Matthew 10:37

IT MAY SEEM odd that family would make the list of idols in America. But family can be a considerable impediment to discovering and fulfilling your God-given life purpose.

I certainly am not adding my voice to the vast numbers who advocate for the dismantling and destruction of

the traditional family. Far too many misguided individuals as well as groups have already jumped on that
bandwagon—with predictable and devastating consequences, I might add.

Statisticians and scientists are quite fond of repeat-
ing the axiom that correlation is not causation. While it
is certainly true that the problems America faces have
many causes, I have no doubt that one of the primary
reasons for societal ruination is the disintegration of
the nuclear family. A thorough investigation of this
phenomenon would require a separate book, but that is
not my purpose here. What I am proposing is that there
are conditions peculiar to some families that inhibit or
prevent members of those families from following the
will of God for their lives. When that happens, family
becomes an idol.

This may not present as significant an issue in much
of Western culture, where individuality is celebrated
and collective behavior is less common. Elsewhere in
the world and within varying subcultures, however, the
need or desire to fulfill familial or cultural expectations
can be drastically intensified.

As I grew older in my college years, I was shocked
to discover just how different my upbringing was. My
family roots were entrenched. Families in that region
of Appalachia often lived in "clannish" situations where
family loyalty was of paramount value. Often the residents of a hollow (holler) or for miles along a creek bore
the family name. Grandparents, grown children and
their children, cousins, aunts, and uncles lived in homes

in what could be referred to as an entire community. The thought of not living with family in such an environment seemed foreign.

I recall a young Asian college student. She excelled academically and seemed to adjust very well to college life here in America. When she announced she would be leaving school after only one year, her fellow students and instructors were hard pressed to understand why. The reason she cited was that her family had given her leave to be gone for only one year, and she did not want to disappoint them or betray their confidence in her by defying their expectations.

This occurs to varying degrees around the world, and America is no exception. This issue does not occur in a vacuum. There are important considerations that must be evaluated. First, some background information is helpful.

When I was still in elementary school, the term *generation gap* began to be used and discussed, not only in scientific literature but in popular culture as well. The expression refers to dissimilar opinions held by different generations regarding things that are of importance to them.

The generation gap is by no means a recent phenomenon. I suppose ancient Greeks and Romans felt much the same as contemporary parents do about how their children value things differently, develop relationships differently, and engage in different forms of activity, entertainment, and communication. Families have always been required to deal with intergenerational change. One notable difference in the twenty-first century is the rapidity with which that change confronts us. In fact, we are living in an age of an exponential explosion of knowledge. For example, from Calvary to the time knowledge doubled in the earth was 1,700 years. Between then and the year 1900, knowledge doubled every one hundred years. By 1945, knowledge was doubling every twenty-five years. By 1982, it was doubling roughly every year. By 2020, it was doubling every twelve hours, or quadrupling every day.[1]

For example, when I was in high school in the early 1970s, typing was an actual class that could be taken as an elective. The typewriters (does anyone remember those?) were primarily manual, but a few were electric, which offered a giant leap in convenience and speed. Rather than writing on the chalkboard, some rooms were equipped with another modern marvel, the overhead projector. Overhead projectors were used to display written material. People listened to music on 8-track cartridges and later on more compact cassette tapes.

Today, people snicker about what were once cutting-edge technologies, since they are now conspicuously old-fashioned. Word processors have replaced typewriters nearly exclusively, boasting capabilities that other generations could not have imagined. Children now learn how to type (or text) before they enter elementary school. Overhead projectors now take up closet space, replaced by smart boards or e-screens. Eight-tracks and cassette tapes are now as uncommon as they once were ubiquitous. Technology allows music and the spoken word to be instantly digitally downloaded to our cell phones anywhere and anytime.

Only equal to the rapid pace of available new technologies is the warp speed with which the chasm between generations is expanding. It is no mystery that today's adolescents, conversant in the latest technology, have diverging ways of relating to each other and the world around them than those of their parents or grandparents.

The telephone hanging on the kitchen wall was once the primary way for teenagers to connect with their peers. It still is, but now it is by means of texting on a cell phone instead of talking. Writing and mailing an actual physical letter (snail mail, as it is now referred to) has been overtaken by burgeoning electronically mediated communication (emails and their offspring), which has the advantage of being sent and received immediately rather than making both parties wait for days or weeks. Penmanship was once not only a symbol of diligence, if not art, but was actually taught in school. And then there is the criminal act of removing cursive writing from our schools altogether in many states. Many students today are unable to read it.

This reveals that generations have historically had a more or less built-in desire to separate themselves from previous generations and distinguish themselves in important ways from their parents. Being the new and improved generation has always been a rite of passage. The generation following mine certainly fits that description. Yet with the zeal of youth one must always balance respect for elders and respect for individuality.

The Bible speaks to the responsibilities of children and parents respectively, such as in Ephesians 6:1–4: "Children, obey your parents in the Lord, for this is right. 'Honor your father and mother,' which is the first commandment with a promise, 'so that it may be well with you and you may live long on the earth.' Fathers, do not provoke your children to anger, but bring them up in the discipline and instruction of the Lord."

I believe one of the greatest sins parents ever indulge in is attempting to live their lives vicariously through their children. We've all felt the embarrassment of watching a Little League father who was never much of an athlete attempt to force his son to be the next Babe Ruth. Come on, dad. Just enjoy this pristine moment with your child. I undoubtedly had an advantage in that regard. My parents never dictated my future. They gave me the liberty to follow my own path—circumscribed, of course, by legal, moral, and ethical boundaries.

I was determined to have a career in law, but God had other plans. In fact, when I announced my intention to follow the Lord's leading to enter the ministry, my mother immediately asked, "Are you sure? That can be a very difficult path. You'd better be sure it's God calling you. If you are, then preparation is not wasted time." There was no overt celebration on her or my father's part, no "Oh, I always knew God would use you!"

I believe my mother reacted the way she did not

because she didn't want me to follow God's plan for my life but because my parents had a front-row seat to the universal privation that had been the standard for the preachers we knew. The pastors we had encountered through the years were wonderful men, but they were not at the top of the economic food chain by any means—if anything, they were at the other end of the spectrum. As any conscientious parent would, my mother was expressing her concern that I might not be able to make a living doing what God called me to do.

From the first moment I began ministering, my parents were my biggest fans and most loyal supporters. Anything I announced as part of the vision for our local church received a full measure of their untiring efforts to move it forward. I cannot imagine the difficulty I would have faced if they had been unsupportive or even indifferent. I am fully aware that many people have had to deal with this exact situation and it has caused them no end of trouble. In some cases it has extinguished their desire to follow God and short-circuited their obedience to the claims of God on their lives.

It is deadly idolatry to pressure your children to conform to your expectations rather than the leadings of God and their own desires. Some families have an unspoken assumption that the children will follow their parents into the family business, profession, or occupation, which may involve a highly skilled profession such as law, medicine, or even ministry. It may be an expectation that the children will continue the family business, even if they have no interest or inclination to pursue it. It may be a family tradition that everyone works in the same industry, for the same company, or in the same occupation. I have known generations of people who worked at the same factory, facility, or location. The thought of a family member working somewhere else or doing something else was akin to betrayal.

In the past, acceptable occupations tended to be more rigidly divided by gender. Men were doctors and lawyers, and women were nurses and teachers. Thankfully those stereotypes have been largely dismantled, but over the years they have kept many people from following their God-given dreams. How many women were forced to forsake their goal of being a missionary—or, for that matter, a truck driver—because "respectable" young women couldn't do those things? How many men were convinced they could not pursue careers in the arts because those weren't occupations that were regarded as "suitable" for men?

Separate generations view similar issues with totally different perspectives. What to do with one's life is a vastly important decision, one that few teenagers are prepared to make. One question adults are fond of asking children is, "What do you want to be when you grow up?" Most young people don't yet possess the answer to that question. They may have a hero or someone they admire, but that doesn't mean they want to follow them in lockstep.

Perhaps you or someone you know discerned God's will and their heart's desire from a young age and knew what they wanted to do with their life, but that is certainly the exception rather than the rule.

This issue can be the most troubling just as adolescents reach a crisis point in their lives. When they are ready to graduate from high school, if they are considering college, they are asked to choose a field of study. The problem is that they don't know what they want to do, so they risk choosing a path they may not want to follow as they gain additional life experience. When this is combined with pressure from parents or other family members to enter a particular career, it can cause a host of problems.

Think about it: How would you feel if you were guaranteed college tuition to study to become a teacher but would be cut off if you pursued any other degree program? Suppose you deeply desired to study music, or medicine, or mathematics?

One young lady, fulfilling her parents' expectations, got to the end of her four-year program and promptly forsook it as soon as she went through her student teaching experience. Just one week of real-life experience in the classroom convinced her that teaching was not right for her—which is what her heart had been consistently telling her for four years.

My pastor and mentor, Dr. Lester Sumrall, often told me, "Another person's head is no place to keep your happiness." Attempting to live up to someone else's plan for you may work as long as circumstances line up in your favor, but what happens when everything goes wrong? The initiative to press through difficulties and

discouragement may vanish if you are following someone else's goal rather than your own.

Many potential college students face the following
scenario or one similar to it. They find out about a
college or university and even attend a function there.
They return home to announce their desire to pursue
their education at that institution, which happens to be
far from their home. Their parents respond with skepti-
cism and even hostility.

Of course there may be legitimate factors that
prevent a student from attending a school that is out
of state or involves premium tuition rates. Parents will
certainly object to paying the bill to send their child to
Party Hearty U. They will rightly resist the notion that
their teenager has to go to a certain college for no other
reason than some high school friends or acquaintances
plan to attend there as well.

Those kinds of considerations aside, why wouldn't
parents want their children to have the best and
most appropriate education available for the career
the student chooses—especially when God is leading
them to pursue it? Children have to fulfill their own
God-given dreams. They should never feel manipulated
into becoming surrogates for their parents' unfulfilled
dreams for them—or in extreme cases, the parents'
dreams for themselves!

You may have heard horror stories that go along
with this. Dad didn't make it as a professional football
player, so he arranges every detail of his son's life to
try to make him one. If anything goes wrong, the son

feels the weight of his father's disapproval. Mom wanted to be a musician, but due to a family tragedy she had to drop out of school. She never completed her education and training. However, she is not going to miss the chance for her daughter to do what she couldn't. Her daughter dutifully studies piano, but her heart's desire is to take flying lessons instead. The daughter knows that if she were to finally confess her distaste for the piano, conflict with her mother would be inevitable.

In some cases a family assumes a child will go to college, but the child is not interested in an academic pursuit. He or she may be attracted to a trade instead. This should never be a reason for family strife or a power struggle. When I have a retaining wall that needs repair, I can think of nothing more necessary than a bricklayer or stonemason who knows his or her craft. Those who hold degrees in law or medicine have my congratulations and respect; however, they are of little help when my septic tank needs pumped or my furnace has stopped working. The lawn care folks are on the top of my list when the grass needs mowed.

You don't need an advanced degree to have a sense of accomplishment and a good reputation. If young people have an inclination or aptitude in an area, as godly parents we must encourage them to pursue their heart's desire and develop it rather than attempting to steer or coerce them into pursuing a different path.

Then there are those narcissistic parents who actually put great effort into sabotaging their children's plans by playing the sympathy card. It sounds like this: "If you go away to school (or get married, or accept a career in some distant city or state), who will take care of me?" There is no doubt that as people begin to live longer, aging issues that no previous generation has faced will become more prevalent. However, parents cannot keep their children on a tether based on what might happen ten or twenty years in the future. God forbid that the fears and frustrations of parents would hold their children hostage, leaving them unable to become the people God has created and purposed for them to be.

Many adult children make willing sacrifices to ensure they are available to care for their aging parents themselves. As sometimes happens, no child (or grandchild) should be made to feel guilty for pursuing his or her own life and interests because a parent (or grandparent) might feel lonely.

Another devastating scenario can manifest when a husband or wife does not fulfill the biblical admonition to leave father and mother and cleave to their spouse. (See Genesis 2:24.) Allow me to state very clearly, without stuttering: When a Christian is married, the most important person in their life, other than the Lord Jesus Christ, is their spouse. Period—hard stop! That is and will remain their first priority before God. Regardless of the honor they give their parents and the love and respect they have for them, anything that interferes with their relationship with their lawful husband or wife is out of divine order and will yield a painful harvest of bitterness and strife.

One of the surest ways I know to damage a marriage

relationship is to side with your parents over your spouse. If that happens consistently, it will not just damage a marriage, it will leave it a casualty on the rocks of ruin. This is the clanging crescendo of idolatry; it must be avoided at all costs and renounced and repented of if it has raised its demonic head.

The problems that arise between spouses in this regard usually do not involve some relatively minor controversy about the length of the draperies, the color of the vehicle, allegiance to a sports team, or what brand of coffee to buy. Reasonable people can generally work through such minor disagreements without seeking to bolster their position by getting more people on their side. What I'm saying is no wife should seek her parents' support for her point of view when she has a disagreement with her husband, neither should a husband defer to his parents' wishes regarding the planning of a family vacation or holiday gathering.

Let me take a moment here to state that I am not advocating that anyone should ever endure any form of abuse. My strong advice to anyone suffering abuse is to take immediate and appropriate action to remove yourself from any and all danger.

Husbands and wives should consider one another. They should strengthen and support one another. Most issues that arise between spouses can be resolved by simply loving and preferring one another and being sensitive to the Holy Spirit as foundational principles. Swallow it. Pride is the strength of idolatry. Become accustomed to using and meaning the words "I'm sorry" and "Will you forgive me?" These are spiritual kryptonite to the strongman of idolatry.

Please don't miss this, as I speak from nearly fifty years of pastoral ministry: most controversies and conflicts are only made worse by involving others who are not in a position to remain impartial.

It is often more than appropriate to incorporate long-standing family traditions into a new home, or to emulate godly characteristics demonstrated by other family members. The apostle Paul commended his protégé Timothy for continuing the tradition of faith that came from his family. Second Timothy 1:5 says, "...remembering the genuine faith that first lived in your grandmother Lois and your mother Eunice and that I am persuaded lives in you also." However, every couple should develop their own traditions and ways of doing things that will not be exactly like those of their parents, grandparents, or anyone else.

To defer to parents' wishes without consulting one's spouse is damaging and should never occur in Christian marriages and homes. Advice from parents can be helpful, but intrusion is just that—deliberately placing oneself into a situation where one is unwelcome or uninvited. A difficult but rewarding paramount and guiding principle for parents to heed is to wait for your children to ask for your advice before giving your opinion or counsel about a matter.

Now, a word about the other side of this perilous issue: Adult children should never consider their parents or grandparents to be a continual and unlimited source of loans, gifts, childcare, lodging, transportation, food, or anything else for that matter. During times of crisis, families will certainly provide help for one another in ways that may not be necessary once the crisis is over. However, the process of maturity means children have increasing independence from parents—they are parents, not gods, and certainly not idols. Along with greater independence from family there must be a correlating dependence upon God, who is the ultimate source of everything we need in this life and the life to come.

There is another idol atop the family mountain. There are times when, sometimes unwittingly, parents hold their children in higher esteem than God, thus making them idols. In many cases they do not realize this is actually what they are doing. Observe the following scenario.

A young person displays an aptitude in some athletic or artistic pursuit. It may be basketball, piano, or any other ability. The parents encourage their child to develop this talent by enrolling them in classes, organizations, or teams that cultivate the child's gift and afford them opportunities to use it. These commitments could interfere with church attendance, spiritual pursuits, or personal devotions. If such a situation goes uncorrected, the child may become proficient in their chosen skill, but they may also become lukewarm or even cold in their spiritual life as a result. Dear reader, this is precisely what the Lord Jesus was getting at in His stern rebuke of Peter for being too mindful of the things of men and thereby forfeiting the more important things of God. (See Matthew 16:23.) Jesus' discourse continues in verses 24–26:

> Then Jesus said to His disciples, "If anyone will come after Me, let him deny himself, and take up his cross, and follow Me. For whoever would save his life will lose it, and whoever loses his life for My sake will find it. For what will it profit a man if he gains the whole world and loses his own soul? Or what shall a man give in exchange for his soul?"

I enjoyed playing organized baseball when I was a boy. One of my team's weekly practices was held on Wednesday nights. My parents went to the coach in private and explained our situation. I never attended those practices because we had church services at 7:00 p.m. on Wednesdays. In the unlikely event that a game was scheduled on a Sunday, I did not play. My parents made it clear to my coach that my relationship with God was more important than my involvement in sports. Because they did so, I understood that having God in my life was their priority. I often share with parents that what your children see you making a priority, they will make a priority.

May we never worship at the idols of temporal pleasure and pursuit and neglect the weightier matters of eternal life through Jesus Christ. Whenever we had a choice to make at our house, it was always decided strongly in favor of learning more about God and experiencing more of the things of God rather than learning more about baseball or other more trivial endeavors.

You may feel that your child is an exception to this principle and is strong enough to resist the pressure to conform that occurs so powerfully in adolescence. I encourage you to make decisions regarding the children given to you by the living God that will guide and encourage them to make decisions themselves that will always keep God in first place at all times. Anything else, no matter how attractive it may seem, is an idol.

Is there any hope? It is not my intention at the end of this narrative regarding idolatry to leave you brokenhearted and empty handed. I am happy to tell you, without equivocation, there is hope. I speak not of generic hope but of that very specific hope based upon a very precise promise given to humanity by the only true and living God. I have lived in that hope since I was eight years of age, and I want to share it with you next.

# EPILOGUE

*Little children, keep yourselves from idols (false gods)—[from
anything and everything that would occupy the place in your
heart due to God, from any sort of substitute for Him that
would take first place in your life]. Amen (so let it be).*
—1 JOHN 5:21, AMPC

WO FRIENDS WERE talking about the state of American culture.

"I have good news and bad news," one said.

"What's the good news?" his friend asked.

"Things are really bad," the first friend replied.

"I know things are bad, but I asked you about the good news."

"That is the good news."

"Are you kidding? If that is the good news, what is the bad news?"

"Things are never so bad that they cannot get even worse."

These two will probably not qualify as candidates for the local Optimists Club, but their assessment of the state of affairs in America is probably shared by most at present. Societal destruction and disintegration proceeds apace, in my opinion, and it is being fueled by idolatry. All idolatry is based upon lies rather than truth, and the coin of truth has been greatly devalued and depreciated in a culture that trades in the currency of dishonesty, disinformation, and deceit.

Multitudes become involved in idolatry without understanding its implications. Others believe that their idol will aid them or produce benefits in their lives. Whether they bow at the altar of their idol of choice as a result of blind ritualism or because they believe their false deity is actually real, the result will be the same. At some point, regardless of whether their worship is legitimate or not, their idol will exact the payment that is due. It will be far higher a price and more devastating an outcome than the deceived worshipper can imagine. Here is an example from God's Word.

Ahab was among the worst of the ungodly kings of Israel, as the northern kingdom became known after it was divided during the realm of Rehoboam. First Kings 21:25–26 records the downfall: "But there were none compared to Ahab, who sold himself to evil deeds in the sight of the LORD, which Jezebel his wife stirred up. He performed the most abominable act in following idols like the Amorites, whom the LORD cast out before the children of Israel."

As a result of his idolatry, Ahab was perhaps the most corrupt of an unbroken litany of corrupt rulers. He assumed that his false gods would insulate him against judgment from the God of heaven. He did attempt to humble himself to some degree following the prophetic words of judgment that Elijah pronounced upon him, but it was too late to avert the sure and mighty hand of God's justice. Here is Elijah's message to Ahab, in part, from 1 Kings 21:19: "Thus says the LORD: In the place where dogs licked the blood of Naboth, dogs will lick your own blood!"

The fulfillment of God's word is recorded in 1 Kings 22:37–38, after Ahab was mortally wounded in battle with the Syrians: "So the king died and was brought to Samaria, and they buried him there. The chariot was washed in the pool of Samaria, and the dogs licked up the king's blood, and they washed his armor according to the word which the LORD spoke."

I wonder just how much blood has already been shed as a result of our nation's abhorrent addiction to idolatry. And I am deeply burdened at the thought of how much more blood will be sacrificed to satisfy the lying abominations of false gods that millions continue to worship and serve.

At some point in the not-too-distant future a regime will arise whose very existence will be based on lies. Its goal will be world domination. We are not there yet, but I believe we are dangerously close to the tipping point. At that moment, destructive events will cascade into a full-blown and unstoppable upheaval that will make what has happened up to now look like a Sunday school picnic.

Worshipping an idol will not be a matter of choice in that day—it will be a matter of coercion. Men and women will be forced to worship the idol or die. Also, the idol will not be one of a person's own choosing but rather that which the administrative state chooses for them. None of the false gods to which the masses have surrendered their lives will be able to deliver them in that day. Revelation 13 describes this time clearly and with great specificity.

Yes, things are really bad, and they are about to get even worse. But that is not the most vital part of this message. In contrast to the vain and abominable idols that have proliferated across the American landscape, there is one true and living God. Every counterfeit only demonstrates the existence of something that is genuine. For every imposter there is the absolute and undeniable reality. His name is Jesus Christ, the Lord of glory. He is coming back to this blue marble planet Earth again, and He will establish His kingdom just as He and the prophets foretold.

However, before that great and glorious day arrives, there will come another day that was also prophesied with great precision and certainty. The prophet Joel saw and described it this way: "And it will be that, afterwards, I will pour out My Spirit on all flesh; then your sons and your daughters will prophesy, your old men will dream dreams, and your young men will see visions. Even on the menservants and maidservants in those days I will pour out My Spirit" (Joel 2:28–29).

The day that God's prophet foresaw is this day, which was confirmed by the apostle Peter on the day of Pentecost. (See Acts 2.) Peter preached a convincing sermon to the assembled crowd, and they asked him what they should do. The apostle did not equivocate in his answer. It was but a single word: "Repent!"

In the event you have found yourself ensnared by any idolatrous web of deceit and bondage as I have described in the previous pages, I encourage you to respond to the apostle Peter's directive—repent, and do so now. Turn quickly, purposefully, and forcefully away from your allegiance to them and now, with equal determination, turn toward the only one true and living God. He will, as He promised, forgive, accept, and receive you.

Dear reader, if you have perhaps realized at this point that you have never accepted Jesus Christ as your Savior, please allow me to invite you to do so now. Simply turn to Him and ask Him to come into your heart. He will, and your life will never be the same.

The living God has graced us with a brief window of opportunity to make an impact before the floodgates of institutionalized idolatry open to overwhelm the earth. Our assignment is very clear in the words of Jesus Himself from Matthew 28:19–20:

> Go therefore and make disciples of all nations, baptizing them in the name of the Father and of the Son and of the Holy Spirit, teaching them to observe all things I have commanded you. And remember, I am with you always, even to the end of the age.

The Lord Jesus realized the impossibility of any one person going to all the world. That is even less likely now, with the world's population exceeding eight billion people. So, think of His instruction in this way—go into all of *your* world and proclaim the good news of the lordship of Jesus Christ to your family and friends, your neighbors, acquaintances, and coworkers. God has already promised that He has poured out the Holy Spirit so that all of us can accomplish this purpose. As we do, we will experience not only a revival but a nation-altering, culture-shaking, world-changing awakening.

I believe that we are on the precipice of the greatest move of the Spirit of God the planet has ever witnessed—and our great God has chosen all of us to be invested and involved in it in these final and most exciting days of human history.

The simplicity of the gospel of Jesus Christ is its power, and its power is its simplicity. Presenting the gospel's message is not complicated, nor was it ever meant to be. It involves four points:

◊ Jesus loves you.

◊ Jesus died for you.

◊ Jesus rose from the dead for you.

◊ Jesus can change your life; He changed mine.

For those in your world who doubt this, you can tell them how Jesus changed your life. You can then assure them He will do the same for them.

You may wonder how you can share redemption's story with those around you who are distracted, suspicious, or wary of anyone who approaches them. The "bait" that attracts people is your kindness. It is included in Galatians 5:22 in a list of godly characteristics that should emanate from every believer. (Some translations render it "gentleness.") Kindness is certainly in short supply in our world that is filled with anger and hatred, hostility and rage. Only love and kindness will cut through the clutter and attract people's attention right away.

Once you have gained a listening ear, you can share your personal story with the person. I don't mean telling your entire testimony from the time you were born. Just share something that Jesus did for you, and assure them that He is willing to do the same for them.

You may be wondering if I really believe that individual Christians sharing their faith with others can make enough of a difference to change the outcome of an entire generation. Let me assure you that I do. Second Chronicles 7:14 is a major reason why: "If My people, who are called by My name, will humble themselves and pray, and seek My face and turn from their wicked ways, then I will hear from heaven, and will forgive their sin and will heal their land." I explained in detail how this will take place in my book entitled *Revival If.*

I encourage you to believe God together with me that the heart of our nation will be turned from dead idols to serve the living God—from temporary things to eternal things. The apostle Paul wrote to his friends in Thessalonica in regard to how their personal testimony affected others in 1 Thessalonians 1:9: "For they themselves declare how we were received by you, and how you turned to God from idols, to serve the living and true God." Second Corinthians 4:18 puts it this way: "While we do not look at the things which are seen, but at the things which are not seen. For the things which are seen are temporal, but the things which are not seen are eternal."

It has happened before, and I am convinced it is happening again—right here, right now. A nation adrift from its moral moorings is turning to the truth and is about to experience a flood of the Holy Spirit of God. Idolatry causes the rain to be withheld, but true repentance releases times of outpouring and refreshing. So says Acts 3:19 (TPT): "And now you must repent and turn back to God so that your sins will be removed, and so that times of refreshing will stream from the Lord's presence. And he will send you Jesus, the Messiah, the appointed one."

I feel as Elijah must have felt as he confronted King Ahab during the last day of a drought that had lasted for more than three years. The land was parched, dusty, and dry, but the outcome was already assured.

Today, my message is the same as Elijah's was, as recorded in 1 Kings 18:41 (MSG): "Rain is on the way; I hear it coming." Can you hear it? An outpouring is about to arrive!

# NOTES

## Chapter 1

1. "Elvis Buys Graceland," *Daily World*, March 24, 1957, https://www.newspapers.com/article/47027058/elvis-buys-graceland/.
2. Peter Guralnick, *Last Train to Memphis: The Rise of Elvis Presley* (London: Little, Brown, 1994), 83.
3. Dictionary.com, s.v. "fan," accessed August 29, 2023, https://www.dictionary.com/browse/fan.
4. Dictionary.com, s.v. "fanatic," accessed September 13, 2023, https://www.dictionary.com/browse/fanatic.
5. Dictionary.com, s.v. "fanatic," accessed September 13, 2023, https://www.dictionary.com/browse/fanatic.
6. Blaise Cendrars, *Hollywood: Mecca of the Movies* (Berkeley, CA: University of California Press, 1995), 23.
7. Cendrars, *Hollywood*.
8. Cendrars, *Hollywood*; "Los Angeles," History.com, February 28, 2019, https://www.history.com/topics/us-states/los-angeles-california.
9. "History of Hollywood, California," US History.com, accessed September 17,

2023, https://www.u-s-history.com/pages/
h3871.html; "The Rise of Hollywood and
the Arrival of Sound," Digital History,
accessed September 17, 2023, https://
www.digitalhistory.uh.edu/topic_display.
cfm?tcid=124.

10. Ohio State Department of Athletics, "Ohio
State Athletics Reports Rebound in Revenue
in 2022," Ohio State News, January 26, 2023,
https://news.osu.edu/ohio-state-athletics-
reports-rebound-in-revenue-in-2022/.

11. Dave Manuel, "Judge Seamus McCaffery
Presided Over 'Eagles Court,'" Sports-King.
com, July 11, 2022, https://www.sports-king.
com/jail-veterans-stadium-philadelphia-3363/.

12. Manuel, "Judge Seamus McCaffery Presided
Over 'Eagles Court.'"

# CHAPTER 2

1. Rose Eveleth, "Hollywood Overvalues
Older Male Actors and Undervalues Older
Women," Smithsonian Magazine, February
7, 2014, https://www.smithsonianmag.
com/smart-news/hollywood-overvalues-
older-male-actors-and-undervalues-older-
women-180949670/.

2. BrainyQuote, "Dolly Parton Quotes,"
accessed September 13, 2023, https://
www.brainyquote.com/quotes/dolly_
parton_446782.

3. Sky Ariella, "28 Dazzling Fashion Industry
Statistics [2023]: How Much Is the Fashion
Industry Worth," Zippia, June 15, 2023,
https://www.zippia.com/advice/fashion-
industry-statistics/.

4. Ariella, "28 Dazzling Fashion Industry Statistics [2023]."

5. Ariella, "28 Dazzling Fashion Industry Statistics [2023]."

6. Giada Nizzoli, "How Many Times Do We Wear Our Clothes? (Not Enough!)," Project Cece, April 6, 2022, https://www.projectcece.com/blog/506/how-many-times-do-we-wear-our-clothes/.

7. Chris Kolmar, "22 Fulfilling Fitness Industry Statistics [2023]: Home Workout and Gym Statistics," Zippia, July 4, 2023, https://www.zippia.com/advice/fitness-industry-statistics/.

8. Eran Galperin, "101 Gym Membership Statistics to Know," Gymdesk, September 2, 2022, https://gymdesk.com/blog/gym-membership-statistics/#chapter02.

9. "What Percentage of Gym Memberships Go Unused?" Exercise.com, August 24, 2023, https://www.exercise.com/grow/unused-gym-memberships-percentage/; Richard Laycock and Catherine Choi, "Americans Spend $397 Million on Unused Gym Memberships Annually," Finder, May 24, 2021, https://www.finder.com/unused-gym-memberships.

10. Allison Lau, "The Rise of Fad Diets," CNBC Make It, January 11, 2021, https://www.cnbc.com/video/2021/01/11/how-dieting-became-a-71-billion-industry-from-atkins-and-paleo-to-noom.html.

11. Lau, "The Rise of Fad Diets."

12. Lau, "The Rise of Fad Diets."

13. Frédéric Michas, "Revenue of Cosmetic Procedures in the US by Type 2022,"

August 31, 2023, https://www.statista.com/statistics/281346/total-revenue-on-cosmetic-procedures-in-the-united-states-by-type/.

14. American Society of Plastic Surgeons, "2020 Plastic Surgery Statistics," accessed September 13, 2023, https://www.plasticsurgery.org/news/plastic-surgery-statistics.

15. BrainyQuote, "Joan Rivers Quotes," accessed September 13, 2023, https://www.brainyquote.com/quotes/joan_rivers_450916.

16. WebMD Editorial Contributors, "Narcissism: Symptoms and Signs," WebMD, March 30, 2023, https://www.webmd.com/mental-health/narcissism-symptoms-signs.

# CHAPTER 3

1. Cullen McCue, "'You Can Buy a Senator': BlackRock Recruiter Details How Financial Firms 'Buy Politicians' in Shocking Video," Trending Politics, June 21, 2023, https://trendingpoliticsnews.com/watch-blackrock-recruiter-details-how-financial-firms-buy-politicians-in-shocking-video-you-can-buy-a-senator-cmc/?utm_source=whatfinger.

2. Israel Salas-Rodriguez, "She's in Tub-ble: Pelosi's Fridge of Posh $12 Ice Cream Blamed for Hampering Dems in Disastrous House Election," The U.S. Sun, November 12, 2020, https://www.the-sun.com/news/1788334/pelosis-fridge-ice-cream-blamed-election/.

3. Mark Moore, "Climate Buster: Biden 'Green Czar' John Kerry's Jet Unleashes Tons of CO2," *New York Post*, updated July 24, 2022, https://nypost.com/2022/07/19/

climate-buster-biden-green-czar-john-kerrys-jet-unleashes-tons-of-co2/.

4. Emily Goodin, "Republican Fabulist George Santos OFFICIALLY Under Ethics Investigation in Congress: House Approves Panel to Probe His Multiple Lies and Misconduct—Including Sexual Misconduct Allegations," DailyMail.com, updated March 3, 2023, https://www.dailymail.co.uk/news/article-11813755/Republican-fabulist-George-Santos-officially-ethics-investigation.html; The Editorial Board, "President Joe Biden's Endless Stream of Lies," February 1, 2023, https://www.dailynews.com/2023/02/01/president-joe-bidens-endless-stream-of-lies/.

5. James A. Garfield, "A Century of Congress," *The Atlantic*, accessed September 15, 2023, https://www.theatlantic.com/magazine/archive/1877/04/a-century-of-congress/519708/.

6. James A. Garfield, in a speech delivered at Ravenna, Ohio, July 4, 1865; Wikiquote, "James A. Garfield," accessed September 15, 2023, https://en.wikiquote.org/wiki/James_A._Garfield.

7. Dan McLaughlin, "Only Some Kinds of Protest Are Always 'Mostly Peaceful,'" National Review, August 27, 2020, https://www.nationalreview.com/corner/only-some-kinds-of-protest-are-always-mostly-peaceful/.

8. *Merriam-Webster*, s.v. "power," accessed September 16, 2023, https://www.merriam-webster.com/dictionary/power.

9. Sarah Scire, "Half of Americans Think Most National News Orgs Intend to Mislead or Misinform the Public, New Report

Finds," Nieman Lab, February 21, 2023, https://www.niemanlab.org/2023/02/half-of-americans-think-most-national-news-orgs-intend-to-mislead-or-misinform-the-public/; Jim Hoft, "Rough Time for Fake News: Trust in Media in the Sewer—Majority of Americans Now Believe Media Intends to 'Mislead, Misinform or Persuade the Public,'" Gateway Pundit, March 15, 2023, https://www.thegatewaypundit.com/2023/03/rough-time-for-fake-news-trust-in-media-in-the-sewer-majority-of-americans-now-believe-media-intends-to-mislead-misinform-or-persuade-the-public/.

10. Tom Slater, "Mark Zuckerberg Won't Kill Twitter," The Spectator, June 20, 2023, https://www.spectator.co.uk/article/mark-zuckerberg-wont-kill-twitter/.

11. Matthew Huff, "OK, But How Much Does a Met Gala Ticket Cost?" Parade.com, May 1, 2023, https://parade.com/entertainment/met-gala-ticket-price.

12. Daisy Jordan, "You Won't Believe How Much Celebs Paid to Attend This Year's Met Gala," Wear Next, May 2, 2023, https://wear-next.com/news/how-much-does-a-ticket-to-the-met-gala-cost/.

# CHAPTER 4

1. Pew Research Center, "The Global Religious Landscape," December 18, 2012, https://www.pewresearch.org/religion/2012/12/18/global-religious-landscape-exec/; Wikipedia, s.v. "Religion," accessed September 16,

2023, https://en.wikipedia.org/wiki/
Religion#Specific_religions.

2. Tracy F. Munsil, "Biblical Worldview Among
U.S. Adults Drops 33 Percent Since Start of
COVID-19 Pandemic," Arizona Christian
University, February 28, 2023, https://www.
arizonachristian.edu/2023/02/28/biblical-
worldview-among-u-s-adults-drops-33-since-
start-of-covid-19-pandemic/.

3. "Quotes of Leonard Ravenhill," The Gospel
Truth, accessed September 16, 2023, https://
www.gospeltruth.net/ravenhill.htm.

# CHAPTER 5

1. Judith A. Reisman and Edward W. Eichel,
*Kinsey, Sex and Fraud: The Indoctrination of
a People* (n.p.: Vital Issues Press, 1990),
abstract viewed at U.S. Department of
Justice Virtual Library, accessed September
17, 2023, https://www.ojp.gov/ncjrs/virtual-
library/abstracts/kinsey-sex-and-fraud-
indoctrination-people.

2. "Kinsey Helped Undermine Laws
Protecting Women and Children,"
StopTheKinseyInstitute.org, accessed
September 17, 2023, https://
stopthekinseyinstitute.org/more/
undermining-laws/.

3. "More Than 64 Million Unborn Children
Have Died Since Roe v. Wade," National
Right to Life, January 20, 2023, https://
www.nrlc.org/communications/more-than-
64-million-unborn-children-have-died-since-
roe-v-wade/.

4.  Jeff Diamant and Besheer Mohamed, "What the Data Says About Abortion in the U.S.," Pew Research Center, January 11, 2023, https://www.pewresearch.org/short-reads/2023/01/11/what-the-data-says-about-abortion-in-the-u-s-2/.

5.  Annalee Newitz, "Yes, Humans Are Animals—So Just Get Over Yourself, *Homo Sapiens*," Gizmodo, June 10, 2014, https://gizmodo.com/yes-humans-are-animals-so-just-get-over-yourselves-1588990060.

6.  Donna Barry and McKinley Sherrod, "Ensuring Access to Sexually Transmitted Infection Care for All," Center for American Progress, October 16, 2014, https://www.americanprogress.org/article/ensuring-access-to-sexually-transmitted-infection-care-for-all/.

7.  American Psychological Association, "A Glossary: Defining Transgender Terms," *Monitor on Psychology* 49, no. 8 (2018): 32, https://www.apa.org/monitor/2018/09/ce-corner-glossary.

8.  LGBTQIA+ Wiki, s.v. "Xenogender," accessed September 17, 2023, https://www.lgbtqia.wiki/wiki/Xenogender.

9.  WebMD Editorial Contributors, "What's the Difference Between Sex and Gender?" WebMD, accessed September 17, 2023, https://www.webmd.com/a-to-z-guides/difference-between-sex-and-gender.

10. Leonard Sax, "How Common Is Intersex? A Response to Anne Fausto-Sterling," *Journal of Sex Research* 39, no. 3 (August 2002): 174–178, https://doi.org/10.1080/00224490209552139.

11.    Jeffrey Walton, "Methodist Drag Queen 'Ms. Penny Cost' Returns in Florida Children's Sermon," Juicy Ecumenism: The Institute on Religion & Democracy's Blog, October 7, 2022, https://juicyecumenism.com/2022/10/07/methodist-drag-queen-ms-penny-cost-returns-in-florida-childrens-sermon/; Emily McFarlan Miller, "First Drag Queen Certified as a Candidate for United Methodist Ministry 'Speaking in a New Way to New People,'" Religion News Service, April 15, 2021, https://religionnews.com/2021/04/15/first-drag-queen-certified-as-a-candidate-for-united-methodist-ministry-speaking-in-a-new-way-to-new-people/; Mark Tooley, "Drag Queens and the Coming Methodist Schism," World News Group, December 8, 2021, https://wng.org/opinions/drag-queens-and-the-coming-methodist-schism-1638971054.

## Chapter 6

1.    "COVID-19: Schools for More Than 168 Million Children Globally Have Been Completely Closed for Almost a Full Year, Says UNICEF," UNICEF, March 2, 2021, https://www.unicef.org/press-releases/schools-more-168-million-children-globally-have-been-completely-closed.

2.    Kirsten Acuna, "George Lucas Was Convinced 'Star Wars' Would Flop and Refused to Believe It Was a Hit Until He Got a Call Telling Him to Turn On the News," Insider, May 4, 2021, https://www.insider.com/when-george-lucas-knew-star-wars-was-a-hit.

3. Phil McCausland and Dan De Luce, "Iran Enriching Uranium to Near Weapons-Grade Levels, Nuclear Watchdog Warns," NBC News, March 8, 2023, https://www.nbcnews.com/news/world/iran-enriching-uranium-weapons-grade-nuclear-iaea-rcna72753.

# CHAPTER 7

1. Dictionary.com, s.v. "covetousness," accessed September 16, 2023, https://www.dictionary.com/browse/covetousness.
2. "Transnational Organized Crime: The Globalized Illegal Economy," United Nations Office on Drugs and Crime, accessed September 16, 2023, https://www.unodc.org/toc/en/crimes/organized-crime.html.
3. "Global Wealth Report 2023," Credit Suisse, accessed September 16, 2023, https://www.credit-suisse.com/about-us/en/reports-research/global-wealth-report.html.
4. Zia Qureshi, "Rising Inequality: A Major Issue of Our Time," Brookings, May 16, 2023, https://www.brookings.edu/research/rising-inequality-a-major-issue-of-our-time/.
5. Christopher Browne, "2022 Commercial Gaming Revenue Tops $60B, Breaking Annual Record for Second Consecutive Year," American Gaming Association, February 15, 2023, https://www.americangaming.org/new/2022-commercial-gaming-revenue-tops-60b-breaking-annual-record-for-second-consecutive-year/.
6. J. B. Maverick, "Why Does the House Always Win? A Look at Casino Profitability," Investopedia, updated

November 29, 2022, https://www.investopedia.com/articles/personal-finance/110415/why-does-house-always-win-look-casino-profitability.asp.

7.  The Investopedia Team, "The Lottery: Is It Ever Worth Playing?" Investopedia, updated January 6, 2023, https://www.investopedia.com/managing-wealth/worth-playing-lottery/.

8.  "How Dangerous Is Lightning?" National Weather Service," accessed September 16, 2023, https://www.weather.gov/safety/lightning-odds.

9.  The Investopedia Team, "The Lottery."

10.  Amelia Josephson, "The Economics of the Lottery in the U.S.," SmartAsset, updated August 25, 2023, https://smartasset.com/taxes/the-economics-of-the-lottery.

11.  Brian O'Connell, "9 of the Biggest Financial Fraud Cases in History," *U.S. News & World Report*, June 13, 2023, https://money.usnews.com/investing/stock-market-news/slideshows/biggest-corporate-frauds-in-history?slide=2; Rohan Goswami and MacKenzie Sigalos, "How Sam Bankman-Fried Swindled $8 Billion in Customer Money, According to Federal Prosecutors," CNBC, updated December 19, 2022, https://www.cnbc.com/2022/12/18/how-sam-bankman-fried-ran-8-billion-fraud-government-prosecutors.html.

12.  O'Connell, "9 of the Biggest Financial Fraud Cases in History."

13.  O'Connell, "9 of the Biggest Financial Fraud Cases in History"; Robert Bryce, "From Enron to the Financial Crisis, With Alan Greenspan in Between," *US News & World Report*,

September 24, 2008, https://www.usnews.com/opinion/articles/2008/09/24/from-enron-to-the-financial-crisis-with-alan-greenspan-in-between.

14. Ken Belson, "Ex-Chief of WorldCom Is Found Guilty in $11 Billion Fraud," *New York Times*, March 16, 2005, https://www.nytimes.com/2005/03/16/business/exchief-of-worldcom-is-found-guilty-in-11-billion-fraud.html; Wikipedia, s.v. "WorldCom Scandal," accessed September 16, 2023, https://en.wikipedia.org/wiki/WorldCom_scandal.

15. O'Connell, "9 of the Biggest Financial Fraud Cases in History."

16. O'Connell, "9 of the Biggest Financial Fraud Cases in History"; Grant McCool and Martha Graybow, "Madoff Pleads Guilty, Is Jailed for $65 Billion Fraud," Reuters, March 12, 2009, https://www.reuters.com/article/us-madoff/madoff-pleads-guilty-is-jailed-for-65-billion-fraud-idUSTRE52A5JK20090313; "5 of the Biggest Financial Scams in US History," Top Accounting Degrees, accessed September 16, 2023, https://www.topaccountingdegrees.org/lists/5-of-the-biggest-financial-scams-in-us-history/.

17. Rod Parsley, *Silent No More* (Lake Mary, FL: Charisma House, 2005), 4–5.

18. NeoMam Studios, "The Median Home Size in Every U.S. State in 2022," Visual Capitalist, November 22, 2022, https://www.visualcapitalist.com/cp/median-home-size-every-american-state-2022/.

19. "US Existing Single-Family Home Median Sales Price," YCharts.com, accessed September 16, 2023, https://ycharts.com/indicators/

us_existing_singlefamily_home_median_sales_
price.

20. "Historical US Home Prices: Monthly
Median From 1953–2023," DQYDJ, accessed
September 16, 2023, https://dqydj.com/
historical-home-prices/#United_States_
Median_Home_Price_History.

21. "Current Credit Card Interest Rates,"
Bankrate, September 13, 2023, https://www.
bankrate.com/finance/credit-cards/current-
interest-rates/.

22. Matt Schulz, "2023 Credit Card Debt
Statistics," LendingTree, updated September
8, 2023, https://www.lendingtree.com/credit-
cards/credit-card-debt-statistics/.

23. Claire Tsosie, "How Credit Card Issuers
Calculate Minimum Payments," NerdWallet,
updated November 28, 2022, https://www.
nerdwallet.com/article/credit-cards/credit-card-
issuer-minimum-payment.

24. Susan Meyer, "Study: Average Car Size Is
Increasing—Will Roads Still Be Safe for Small
Cars and Pedestrians?" The Zebra, updated
August 31, 2023, https://www.thezebra.com/
resources/driving/average-car-size/.

25. Priscilla Aguilera, "13 Ways to Increase Your
Car's Value," GOBankingRates, May 3, 2021,
https://www.gobankingrates.com/saving-
money/car/how-increase-car-value/?utm_
campaign=949461&utm_source=yahoo.
com&utm_content=16.

26. "What Is the National Debt?" Fiscal Data,
Treasury.gov, accessed September 16, 2023,
https://fiscaldata.treasury.gov/americas-
finance-guide/national-debt/.

# CHAPTER 8

1.  Wikipedia, s.v. "Medieval Warm Period," accessed September 16, 2023, https://en.wikipedia.org/wiki/Medieval_Warm_Period; Wikipedia, s.v. "Little Ice Age," accessed September 16, 2023, https://en.wikipedia.org/wiki/Little_Ice_Age.

2.  Ross McKitrick, "Putting the 'Con' in Consensus; Not Only Is There No 97 Per Cent Consensus Among Climate Scientists, Many Misunderstand Core Issues," Fraser Institute, May 2015, https://www.fraserinstitute.org/article/putting-the-con-in-consensus-not-only-is-there-no-97-per-cent-consensus-among-climate-scientists-many-misunderstand-core-issues.

3.  John McClaughry, "McClaughry: Is Climate Science Settled? Absolutely Not," Vermont Biz, July 27, 2021, https://vermontbiz.com/news/2021/july/27/mcclaughry-climate-science-settled-absolutely-not.

4.  Deborah D'Souza, "Understanding the Green New Deal and What's in the Climate Proposal," Investopedia, updated May 28, 2022, https://www.investopedia.com/the-green-new-deal-explained-4588463.

5.  Andrew Gumbel, "Train to Nowhere: Can California's High-Speed Rail Project Ever Get Back on Track?" *The Guardian*, May 29, 2022, https://www.theguardian.com/us-news/2022/may/29/california-high-speed-rail-bullet-train.

6.  Gary L. Francione and Anna E. Charlton, "The Case Against Pets," Aeon, September 8, 2016, https://aeon.co/essays/

why-keeping-a-pet-is-fundamentally-unethical. For more information, see Wesley J. Smith's book *A Rat Is a Pig Is a Dog Is a Boy: The Human Cost of the Animal Rights Movement,* available on Amazon, https://www.amazon.com/Rat-Pig-Dog-Boy-Movement/dp/1594033463?asin=1594033463&revisionId=&format=4&depth=1.

7.  Wikipedia, s.v. "Timeline of Animal Liberation Front Actions," accessed September 16, 2023, https://en.wikipedia.org/wiki/Timeline_of_Animal_Liberation_Front_actions.

8.  Katherine J. Wu, "Plants May Let Out Ultrasonic Squeals When Stressed," Smithsonian, December 9, 2019, https://www.smithsonianmag.com/smart-news/scientists-record-stressed-out-plants-emitting-ultrasonic-squeals-180973716/.

# Chapter 9

1.  Wikipedia, s.v. *"Lunch Atop a Skyscraper,"* accessed September 16, 2023, https://en.wikipedia.org/wiki/Lunch_atop_a_Skyscraper.

2.  National Park Service, "'The Greatest Dam in the World': Building Hoover Dam (Teaching with Historic Places)," accessed September 16, 2023, https://www.nps.gov/articles/-the-greatest-dam-in-the-world-building-hoover-dam-teaching-with-historic-places.htm.

3.  Koni Nordmann Concepts, "1984: Statue of Liberty," accessed September 16, 2023, https://koninordmann.ch/en/home/liberty/.

4. Wikipedia, s.v. "lawfare," accessed September 15, 2023, https://en.wikipedia.org/wiki/Lawfare.

5. "U.N. World Water Development Report 2023," UNESCO, accessed September 17, 2023, https://www.unesco.org/reports/wwdr/2023/en.

6. Leonard Ravenhill, *Why Revival Tarries* (Minneapolis: Bethany House, 1987), 82.

# CHAPTER 10

1. Scott Sorokin, "Thriving in a World of "Knowledge Half-Life," CIO, April 5, 2019, https://www.cio.com/article/219940/thriving-in-a-world-of-knowledge-half-life.html; Patrice Lewis, "Is Knowledge Doubling—or Halving?" WND, May 27, 2016, https://www.wnd.com/2016/05/is-knowledge-doubling-or-halving/.

# ABOUT THE AUTHOR

**D**R. ROD PARSLEY, a statesman, educator, and inspirational preacher, is a best-selling author of more than one hundred books and is the senior pastor of World Harvest Church in Columbus, Ohio. He oversees all the church's major ministries, including Bridge of Hope Missions, Valor Christian College, City Harvest Network, and the *Breakthrough* broadcast, a television program aired globally and seen by millions.

A highly sought-after crusade and conference speaker, he uses his platform to call people to Jesus Christ through the good news of the gospel. His direct style will encourage you to examine your walk with God and strive for excellence in everything you do. He is a fearless champion of an authentic gospel, and he has a passion for loving God and loving people by winning the lost and discipling those who have come into the kingdom.

He and his wife, Joni, have two adult children, Ashton and Austin, as well as a veritable army of spiritual sons and daughters around the world.

To learn more about Dr. Rod Parsley and the many ministries he oversees, please visit www.RodParsley.com, where you can find updates, contact information, and twenty-four-hour access to prayer partners.